ALPHA

ALPHA

THE END OF THE DINOSAURS

JACK SCHNEIDER

NEW DEGREE PRESS

ALPHA

The End of the Dinosaurs

ISBN   978-1-64137-331-9 *Paperback*

            978-1-64137-642-6 *Ebook*

CONTENTS

PREFACE

———

The Mesozoic era, also called the Age of Dinosaurs, spans the period of time on Earth from 250-65 million years ago (MYA). There are three periods in the Mesozoic era:

- The Triassic (250-201 MYA)
- The Jurassic (201-145 MYA)
- The Cretaceous (145-65 MYA)

Dinosaurs appeared about 220 MYA in the middle of the Triassic and went extinct 65 MYA, at the end of the Cretaceous. The majority of this story takes place 65 MYA, but other time periods are discussed.

The Triassic is preceded by the Permian period, when the Earth was dominated by creatures called mammal-like reptiles. Dinosaurs became the dominant creatures on Earth after the Triassic. The Cretaceous is followed by the Paleogene period, which is divided into epochs. The Paleogene was when mammals began to flourish and evolve. The Permian and the second epoch of the Paleogene, the Eocene (56-34 MYA) are all discussed in the story.

Any paragraphs in italics contain more scientific information that is interesting and relevant to the story. They are, in a sense, part of your story, but serve a different purpose.

It should be noted that any possible errors are mine and mine alone, but all of this information should be up to date as of 2019.

With this information, the story can be more easily enjoyed. Let the journey begin.

INTRODUCTION

"Millions of years of predatory instinct engraved in her DNA, and only one, the most primal, rings true in Alpha's head: Run."

This was the first sentence that came to me while I was planning out this project. I loved it. It's one of those sentences that sounds so good in your head that it would drive a writer to do something with it, even if it never turns into a full novel.

To understand where the idea for this story came from, we need to go back. Not as far as the dinosaur era, but as far as my senior year in high school. During that year in my English class, we were given an assignment to write an informative essay. It could be about any subject we wanted. Naturally, I chose dinosaurs.

I knew what I wanted to do with my life very early on. I love dinosaurs. As a child, I watched many documentaries on TV and had countless dinosaur encyclopedias that I would flip through. The most interesting facts would stick with me and when I would present them to other people, they would ask: "*How do you know this?*"

The answer is simple: Because it's fascinating. These were the biggest, fiercest, and most successful creatures to ever live on the planet and they spark a wonder in me that is hard to explain. I can run my finger over some of the fossils in my collection and trace the impressions left behind by a trilobite's exoskeleton or place my finger tip on the edge of a *Megalodon* tooth and imagine the creature that carried it. These rocks were once alive and I feel I can breathe the ancient air and see the creatures they belonged to as they must have been an unfathomable amount of time ago.

So yes, I chose dinosaurs. In fact, I chose mass extinctions. My plan with the essay was to write about the biggest mass extinction, the end-Permian, and then the most famous one, the end-Cretaceous, and relate them to the climate change happening today. The Big Five mass extinctions were caused by a large amount of carbon dioxide being pumped into the atmosphere by tectonic activities and possible impacts from space. By studying the events that followed and why certain creatures went extinct, we can make predictions about what might happen if humans continue down their path of destruction.

The word minimum for the essay was 2,000 and the max was 2,500. I hit 2,500 halfway through discussing the Cretaceous extinction. I went back through the essay and was forced to cut some of it out and abridge what I had left to discuss to stay within a reasonable range of the word limit (I still turned in a slightly longer essay than the teacher was expecting). I hadn't even gotten around to talking about modern times and had to cut that completely. But overall, I was still proud of how the essay turned out.

The final project of the year was to take one of the essays we had written that year and turn it into something else. The top suggestion was to make a short video. Following that was to draw a graphic novel, and after that was to make a magazine and be creative with adding pictures. I thought I was stuck. I have no video editing skills, I can barely draw stick figures, and I don't read magazines. But then I realized there is one thing I can do: write. I decided to turn my essay about mass extinctions into a short story. And so the character of Alpha was born.

This short story that I turned in for the project was about ten thousand words. It was basically a first draft of what could turn into a novel. "Someday, maybe," I told myself. I love to write and I have many documents saved on my computer of ideas for books that I had and want to get around to finishing. Someday, I would publish something.

The opportunity came much sooner than expected and during my first year of college, I began to turn this passion into a book. I decided to share Alpha's story and the story of the end of the dinosaurs with the world.

Alpha started out as a *Dromaeosaurus* and then became an *Atrociraptor* as I did more research and interviews and learned that *Dromaeosaurus* might not have been around in the time period I was writing about. Then she became an *Acheroraptor* when I learned that this species had been discovered in the Hell Creek Formation and was almost certainly around at the time of the extinction.

Acheroraptor is now on my list of favorite dinosaurs because of this (other top contenders include *T. rex*, *Ceratosaurus*, and *Gastonia*, if you're curious). I feel there might be a stigma around dinosaurs that they are something for children, or that they were nothing more than big, stupid lizards. One of the goals of this story is to show why people become paleontologists and why I'm studying to become one as well as the true image of the dinosaurs. They ruled the Earth for 160 million years and there's a reason for that. They couldn't have done it by being big, stupid lizards.

The other goal of this story is to show what actually happened the fateful day the asteroid struck the Earth and altered the course of history, and paint a realistic depiction of what happened after. As you read this, I want you to keep in mind that everything presented here is indeed a theory. This is the best theory we currently have for what happened. It has been constructed after watching multiple documentaries, reading books, and talking to experts in the field.

I had the pleasure of sitting down with and interviewing my professor Dr. Penny Higgins and talking to her about Cretaceous mammals. I have learned a lot from her, especially considering that she is also a writer herself. I also was fortunate enough to be able to speak to paleontologists Dr. Jim Kirkland and Dr. Thomas Carr on the phone as well as have email conversations with Dr. Thomas Holtz, Jr. and Dr. Philip Currie. These people are truly amazing paleontologists and deserve all the respect in the world for their contributions to the field. I spoke to biology instructor Randall Ott who was also my high school teacher and one of the smartest people I know. We spoke about animal behavior and by discussing some characteristics of the creatures I was writing about to him, he was able to relate them to modern animals so we could infer about some of their behaviors.

If you're ready, then let's take a walk through the woods 65 million years ago in what will become southern Canada. It's time to go meet Alpha and her pack and discover the world of the Late Cretaceous.

Let's begin . . .

CHAPTER ONE

THE HUNT

———

ACHERORAPTOR

Meaning "savage thief" or "hell's plunderer"
Family: Dromaeosaur (Raptors)
Length: 9.5 feet
Height at hips: Unknown
Weight: 100 pounds
Time Period: Late Cretaceous
Deep snout, suggesting a stronger bite force

EDMONTOSAURUS

Meaning "lizard from Edmonton"
Family: Hadrosaur (Duckbills)
Length: 40 feet

Height at hips: 10 feet
Weight: 3-4 tons
Time Period: Late Cretaceous
Largest duckbill ever discovered in North America

TYRANNOSAURUS REX

Meaning "tyrant lizard king"
Family: Tyrannosaur
Length: 40 feet
Height at hips: 15 feet
Weight: 6-7 tons
Time Period: Late Cretaceous
Round serrated teeth, made to crush bone

A herd of *Edmontosaurus* are grazing on an open field. These dinosaurs are called hadrosaurs, or more commonly, duckbills. They are named for their distinctive mouth structure, resembling a duck's bill; however, unlike the modern duck, the inside of their mouths are lined with teeth. There is a distinctive row like most animals, but teeth also line their cheeks. This is for grinding up the tough plants they eat.

The *Edmontosaurus* walk around on all fours, but have the ability to rear onto their hind legs to run or reach higher leaves. They are also a noisy bunch. The plains echo with their calls, distinctive from other duckbill species. These are calls of socialization, saying that there are ferns over here, or the young ones are over there, or declaring an all-clear signal from those that look into the surrounding trees, wary of predators.

A couple of juvenile males are head-butting each other playfully. They rear onto their back legs to grapple with each other briefly before crashing back down onto all fours. They don't realize it, but they are practicing for when they will compete with each other and other males for mates. This herd is mostly female, save for the adolescents. When these two young males are old enough, they will be forced out of the herd and might form a bachelor group of six or seven other young males to band together for survival.

This behavior has become ingrained in their DNA. Many generations ago, young males who behaved like this became more likely to get a mate and pass on their genes. Now, most juveniles will engage in play like this in preparation for when they grow up.

A grunt of annoyance from one of the adults sends a juvenile scurrying as he clips her leg with his tail. The young ones gallop a little further to the edge of the herd. Their mothers do not question it as the calls of other adults continue to give the all-clear signal, oblivious to the dangers around them. The wind is in favor of the silent hunters watching from the trees.

Sitting in the shade on a rock is a green and brown speckled lizard. He is cooling himself down before he heads into the sun glaring on the plain to look for food. The Late Cretaceous period is not as hot as the earlier Jurassic, when there were no ice caps at the poles, but the global temperature is still higher than today.

The lizard's eyes droop as he enjoys the shade, but a whisper from the ferns on the forest floor alerts him to possible danger. Unwilling to risk anything, his claws immediately find the rock beneath him and he scurries into the bushes. Only a second later, two clawed feet drop down where the lizard was resting. The predator lands silently as she lowers her head to see the frolicking duckbills on the plain. The feathers on her spine stand up a little, signaling her accomplices to remain still.

The predator's green eyes dart around and eventually settle on the two young *Edmontosaurus* that have wandered from the adults. Her tail flicks to the left and its orange feathers shift. Now her pack has spied the juveniles as well.

She is an *Acheroraptor*, with the name meaning "savage thief." She and the rest of her pack stand at nine and a half feet long and weigh about a hundred pounds. Her mouth is full of sickle-shaped serrated teeth, perfect for biting prey and causing the most amount of damage. Her jaws are deeper compared to other dromaeosaurs, suggesting she has a stronger bite force than other species. Raptors like her may have been evolving to use their jaws more often. But they each carry the trademark giant claw on their second toe that needs to be held off the ground. It is perfect for tearing into the sides of their prey.

The female *Acheroraptor* leaps silently back to the forest floor. She starts moving slowly around the trees for a prime position to leap out at the young herbivores, who are still playing, completely unaware of the danger. The raptor doesn't think in words like we do. Instead, her mind is full of images, sounds, and scents. She has hunted young *Edmontosaurus* before and knows exactly how to direct her pack.

We can call her Alpha, because that's how she thinks of herself, although the word is unfamiliar to her. She looks at the rest of her pack waiting farther back in the trees. Most of them are related to her in some way. Her sister, Delta, is among them along with her mate and a couple of their children. There is another female that joined the pack a few years ago as well. Alpha's mate, the Beta of the pack, strides forward to stand next to her. When breeding season arrives for the raptors, there might be a standoff between Beta and the other male in the pack, Delta's mate. Raptors are not sentimental. There might also be challenges from lone males that approach the pack, seeking to improve their social position.

For now, the other raptors stay behind Beta and follow Alpha's lead. She leads the pack slowly around to where the young duckbills are. Alpha waits a moment to make sure they are still unnoticed. But then the wind changes and Alpha's feathers are brushed by the breeze. They cover her entire body to provide insulation as well as other uses for a hunt.

The young duckbills stop as they catch a new scent in the wind. They have never encountered raptors before. At first, they are curious, but then fear grips them. Instinct engraved in their DNA tells them they are no longer safe.

Alpha chirps, almost like a bird, to give the signal to charge. They need to go before the adults catch the scent of the predators or the young hadrosaurs run away. Two raptors race out onto the plain. By spreading their feathers and hissing as loud as they can, they suddenly seem much bigger than they actually are. They are positioned back-to-back between the young dinosaurs, trying to scare one duckbill away and forcing the other one into the forest. They both succeed.

One *Edmontosaurus* runs back to the herd and the other runs into the forest where the pack lies in wait. Two raptors leap onto their prey's side as it passes while the others race along by its feet, nipping at it. They are doing everything they can to lure the juvenile dinosaur, and he has no idea what their plan is. He is just trying to get away. He has reared onto his hind legs to run and is crashing through the forest. He will never outrun the raptors. Not only are they faster, but this is their territory. They know it as well as the feathers on their arms. His only hope is to use his size and his powerful tail to kill enough raptors so that the pack gives up.

Alpha watches the pack and their prey go, with Beta taking the lead. She turns to pursue them, but is stopped by the loud bleating of an adult *Edmontosaurus*. She turns around to see one charging across the plain. The other two raptors on the plain notice it as well. Alpha knows her pack is no match for a forty-foot-long *Edmontosaurus*, the biggest of all the hadrosaurs in North America. She lets out a low guttural call to bring the two raptors back. Once they pass her, she follows them. She does not look back. She knows the adult *Edmontosaurus* will never follow them into the thick forest.

Alpha and the two raptors follow the screams of the young duckbill, the roars of the pack, and the scent of blood to find the hunt again. They weave through the trees as fast as their muscular legs can carry them, at speeds of up to forty miles per hour. Alpha skids to a halt once she passes the scent markers of her pack and sees that Beta has done well giving directions to the other raptors.

The pack has lured their prey into a kill zone. The young duckbill stands in the middle of a gully, the walls higher than he stands. The raptors stand at either side, waiting for the signal from Alpha to attack. She is one of the last to arrive.

Two of the raptors stand with their feathers fluffed up to keep the *Edmontosaurus* from bolting. Alpha leaps into action, landing on the duckbill's neck, and Beta follows, attacking on the side. The raptors are practicing the tried and true slash-and-dash technique, where one raptor runs in and leaps onto the side of the duckbill, slashing and biting to cause as much damage as possible as quickly as they can, then leaps off the prey and races back up the slope, out of harm's way.

As Alpha and Beta leap off the duckbill, the other raptors begin their assault by mimicking their superiors, attacking the same places they did. They take turns leaping at the throat, the most vulnerable part of the animal. If one of them gets lucky, they could sever a major artery with their claws.

With a couple raptors on the side of the duckbill at any one time, he is disoriented and starting to feel the effects of blood loss. He swings his tail as much as he can, hoping to catch a raptor off guard, but they stay away from it. There is not much he can do, and the raptors only need to wait for him to collapse and then they'll have a feast.

A screech of fear catches Alpha's attention. The duckbill has reared up onto his hind legs, revealing a raptor underneath it, paralyzed by fear, knowing that the duckbill might come crashing down, surely killing it. Alpha runs to help, but another raptor gets there first. Alpha recognizes her as one of Delta's children, born a few years ago and now a mature adult. She leaps onto the hadrosaur's face to distract him. He lets out a high pitched call and starts to shake his head to get the raptor off. The raptor underneath the hadrosaur's front legs darts away. Alpha knows that raptor, too. She had a job to do and she failed.

Alpha starts to follow her, but is distracted by the movement of the hadrosaur in the corner of her eye. She turns to see him fling the raptor on his face away. The raptor's body slams into a tree with the sickening crack of multiple brittle and hollow bones snapping. One of her nieces is dead, but there is no sentiment or grief. The pack slows down the attack, but only because they are starting to fear for their own lives. Beta is the first to launch a renewed strike against the duckbill and the rest of the raptors follow his lead.

The death of a pack member is all too common. Alpha is not sad, but is now focused on the actions of the other raptor who caused this. Not because she caused the death of a pack member, but because she left her post of guarding the chicks. This raptor can be called Omega, because she is at the bottom of the social order. Omega was the former alpha of the pack, now reduced to picking off the scraps the rest of the pack leaves behind.

Alpha finds her a short distance away, checking on the chicks. With a roar, Alpha tackles the adult raptor and pins her to the ground. This is not revenge--this is punishment for leaving her post. Omega lets out a startled cry as Alpha forces her head into the dirt with a clawed foot, holding it there for a second and then releasing her. Without hesitation, Alpha returns to the attack. Omega has been punished sufficiently for the moment, and her pack needs her.

The young *Edmontosaurus* is getting tired, and Alpha senses that the end of the hunt is drawing closer.

But then the ground shakes. Alpha's feathers start to prick up as she looks further down the gully. She knows from experience that something big is approaching.

A deafening roar splits the air. It's louder than a 747 airplane taking off. Alpha gives a high-pitched shriek to tell her pack to back off the duckbill. There is something bigger and much more dangerous to contend with.

Another roar comes from farther down the gully. The stomping of massive feet can now be heard by every single raptor. Taking advantage of the distraction, the duckbill lets out a confused cry and starts to limp away from the kill zone and the roar.

A *Tyrannosaurus rex* bares her teeth at the raptors hiding in the trees. She is a huge female seeking her next meal for herself and for the young waiting in her nest back in her territory. With her incredible sense of smell, the scent of hadrosaur blood filled her nose from miles away. When she arrived, she expected to find a dead dinosaur, but instead finds the injured duckbill and Alpha's pack. She gives another massive roar.

For the briefest of instants, Alpha considers ordering her pack to attack the tyrannosaur. But thousands of generations before her have always kept to one rule, if nothing else: Never attack a *T. rex*. The instinct is too strong, and with a chirp, she orders her pack to retreat into the trees. The tyrannosaur will not follow them there.

Alpha hears a crash and sees that the young *Edmontosaurus* has found the strength to rear onto two legs and run. Although his side is stained red from blood loss, he could still recover from these wounds.

The tyrannosaur grunts and then sets off after the duckbill. She is unwilling to spend any energy running and instead settles for steady walk. She is confident in her ability to track the duckbill down once he finds a place to spend the night. The sun is growing low in the sky.

With the tyrannosaur out of sight, Alpha tips her head back and lets out a guttural call to regroup the pack. She is also confident in her pack's ability to track the duckbill. *Acheroraptor* like Alpha are equipped with night vision, and so she plans to remount the attack once the sun has dipped below the horizon. For now, the mother of the chicks heads up the hill to meet Omega and check on her young, while Alpha and Beta settle down next to each other to conserve energy and wait for darkness.

ACHERORAPTOR *JAWS*

Acheroraptor *is known only from fossil parts of the upper and lower jaws. While it was a member of the raptor family,* Acheroraptor *and the closely related* Atrociraptor *share many characteristics with* Saurornitholestes *and its line from Asia. What was previously thought to be teeth from three different species in the Hell Creek Formation that spans the states of Montana, Wyoming, and the Dakotas are now all thought to be from* Acheroraptor.

With the deep snout, Acheroraptor *and* Atrociraptor *are sometimes called the "bulldogs" of the raptors. They probably had a stronger bite force than their ancestors, showing that raptors were growing to be more reliant on their jaws at the end of the reign of the dinosaurs.*

HOLLOW BONES

Raptors and some other carnivorous dinosaurs have been proven to have hollow bones. This makes them lighter so they can run faster and, in the case of raptors, jump higher. But they are also more susceptible to breaking. Even some huge carnivores like Albertosaurus, a slightly smaller relative of T. rex, have been proven to have hollow bones. Most raptor species have them, and so it is likely that Acheroraptor did as well.

CHAPTER TWO

THE NIGHT ATTACK

———

Night falls, and the raptors are on the move again. Setting off down the gully in the direction the duckbill and tyrannosaur went, Alpha puts her nose to the ground and finds the blood trail left by the wounded dinosaur. She screeches a clear message to her pack: "*Follow me.*"

Beta stands a little ways back but still at Alpha's side, ready to keep the pack in order while she leads. This time, Omega follows in the rear of the hunting party. The mother of the chicks has been left with the task of guarding them.

As they move through the night, Alpha is on high alert. Before today, she has only seen one other tyrannosaur and it was from a distance. She wants to do everything she can to avoid her. Her pack is no match for the might of a *T. rex.*

The raptors walk silently across the forest floor, the feathers on their feet muffling any sound they make. Alpha's nose follows the scent of hadrosaur blood while her arms spread and her feathers move like an owl's wings to funnel noises to her ears. She's searching for the distress calls of a certain *Edmontosaurus*.

Soon enough, the smell of the wounded dinosaur becomes much stronger and the pack finds a grove of trees where he must have found shelter for the night.

Alpha's steps and the movements of her feathers and her tail are clear signals to the pack. A couple start giving calls to scare and disorient the hadrosaur. He remains silent, but through the trees, Alpha can see the way his head snaps back and forth, waiting for the attack.

Obeying Alpha's command, Beta leads two raptors around the grove to attack from one side while Delta remains with a few more to attack from the other. With that, Alpha has an idea for herself. There is a large rock that the *Edmontosaurus* has backed himself up to. Instinct tells him that to do so will eliminate a side the raptors can strike from, but Alpha knows a way around it.

In a couple of leaps, she is on top of the rock. Her night vision seeks out the members of her pack to see if they're in position. She is ready to launch a silent, aerial attack.

Once she sees that everyone is ready, she gives a screech and launches herself at the duckbill. He lets out a stunned bellow as he feels Alpha's razor-sharp claws digging into his neck. The pack storms from their hiding places and take advantage of the duckbill's confusion to dig their claws in as deep as they can and reopen all the wounds from earlier in the day.

Now the duckbill is bleeding more than before. In the confined space of the grove, his powerful tail is useless. He tries to swing his greater bulk around and catch a raptor by surprise, but they can see much better than him, and they dodge his attacks with ease. He is no match for these highly-trained killers. Instincts take over as he fights for his life.

After several minutes of these attacks, the duckbill finally collapses onto his side. He has lost too much blood and fallen unconscious. Every single pack member waits. It is Alpha's duty to deal the final blow. She grasps the duckbill's throat in her mouth and bites, crushing his windpipe. Finally, the hunt is completed, and it is time for the raptors to refuel all the calories they burned.

Alpha goes directly to the side of the body and tears into it. She pushes her nose in. She is searching for a soft organ like the liver, knowing that they are the most nutritious parts of the duckbill, her claim as Alpha of the pack. Beta stands behind her, and when she drags the liver away, he begins to feed on the other tastier portions. Delta joins him. The remaining raptors take up their feeding positions. A few fights break out over some parts of the body, but there are no serious injuries. Omega settles for nibbling on the tough flesh of the tail.

Alpha finishes the liver and then turns back for more, when all of a sudden the ground starts to shake in much the same way it did before. Fear overcomes her once again. One of the trees in the grove is pushed over as the female tyrannosaur crashes her way through with a mighty roar. She has smelled the hadrosaur blood once again and knows that the raptors have located their prey.

With another chirp, Alpha reluctantly tells her pack to withdraw once again. The tyrannosaur has won this round simply by showing up. She is over at the carcass in a single step. When she feeds, she will tear off much larger chunks of flesh than the raptors, swallowing everything, including bones, until nothing remains. Her mouth is full of round, serrated teeth made to crush bone. No other animal has teeth like the *T. rex*.

She leans over to grab the carcass in her mouth. She can bite with over ten thousand pounds of pressure. Though she does not exactly feel unsafe being outside her territory, she will still drag the carcass back inside her boundaries to eat and to feed her young. Her strong neck muscles allow her to carry the body in her jaws.

She stomps away back to her own territory, leaving most of the raptor pack half-full. Alpha begins to lead them back to their territory where the chicks and their mother are waiting. Some, including Omega, will have to settle in for a hungry night.

CHAPTER THREE

T. REX AND *NANOTYRANNUS*

——

NANOTYRANNUS

Meaning "pygmy tyrant"
Family: Tyrannosaur
Length: 16 feet
Height at hips: 6.5 feet
Weight: 1 ton
Time Period: Late Cretaceous
Smaller and faster than T. rex; pack hunter

To truly understand the Late Cretaceous, we must look at it through the eyes of more than one species of dinosaur.

The female tyrannosaur's head starts to bow as she passes the scent markers to her territory. The weight of the duckbill's body has tired her. One of the body's feet begins to drag on the ground as she marches onward.

Her scent markers become even stronger as she nears her nesting area. Through the smell of duckbill blood and her young, another smell fills her nostrils. She drops the duckbill instantly. There is something else to deal with. There is one dinosaur a mother *T. rex* fears, and that predator is here.

She opens her mouth and a monstrous roar explodes out of it. It is heard by every dinosaur in or near her territory. In a few huge steps, she moves around the trees shading her nesting area and finds what she feared. One of her young is dead, its throat torn out and its blood soaking the soil. Another has fallen to the ground, injured, while the other two are squaring off against two dinosaurs they have never seen before.

Standing at six and a half feet tall, sixteen feet long, and weighing a ton each are two dinosaurs called *Nanotyrannus*. They turn their attention away from the juvenile tyrannosaurs as the mother approaches. They had found the unguarded young ones and decided to take advantage of easy prey. Now they are shocked and terrified by the mother tyrannosaur's presence. Their fighting experience gave them an edge against the young ones, but the mother's size makes that useless.

The tyrannosaur has met these dinosaurs before. She gives another roar. To her, they are nothing but nuisances. Instinct tells her that she must protect her young at all costs from these dinosaurs. With one giant step, she places herself in-between her young and the two *Nanotyrannus*. With only a snap of her jaws, the two *Nanotyrannus* turn around and race away. Because of their size and the relative length of their legs, they will outrun the mother tyrannosaur, and so she does not bother chasing them.

She turns her attention back to her surviving offspring. With a sniff, she checks that the two still standing are unharmed and watches the wounded one get to his feet. He will survive his wound.

The adult *T. rex* feels no sadness at the death of one of her chicks. Her intelligence is comparable to that of a modern crocodile, and her dinosaur brain isn't capable of mourning. She will take care of her offspring for a while and then send them on their way. Her kind is not intelligent enough for complex pack hunting like the raptors.

She laid many eggs a few seasons ago and has lost many offspring. Some eggs didn't hatch, other chicks were too weak to survive, and some wandered away from the nesting area and were eaten by predators. Not all three of her remaining offspring will make it to adulthood. But for now, the mother has succeeded in driving away the predators.

T. REX PACKS

Some relatives of T. rex, *like* Albertosaurus, *have been found in family groups of individuals of many different ages, so it is possible that* T. rex, *took care of their young and lived in packs.*

THE NANOTYRANNUS MYSTERY

Some paleontologists are still unsure if Nanotyrannus *is a separate species of dinosaur. There is a theory that the supposed* Nanotyrannus *specimens are actually juvenile* T. rex. *Previously, the only known specimens were an unidentified skull from a carnivorous dinosaur and a possible half of a skeleton that was also thought to be a young* T. rex, *nicknamed Jane. But recently, paleontologists have found another skeleton named "Bloody Mary" that was next to a* Triceratops *skeleton. The fossil is still privately owned and so only a select few paleontologists have had the opportunity to study it*[1].

They have so far unearthed the arms of Bloody Mary and compared them to those of an adult T. rex *and found that every single bone was longer in Bloody Mary's arms, despite the fact that the unidentified predator was less than half the size of a* T. rex. *Some paleontologists are considering Bloody Mary a* Nanotryannus, *and they may in fact be right.*

---

1   *Dino Death Match*, Documentary (National Geographic, 2011).

There are a few features that might set Nanotyrannus *apart besides Bloody Mary's arms.* Nanotyrannus *has more teeth sockets in its jaw as well as a longer snout. It may have also held its head differently than* T. rex *and had longer legs proportionally, making it more adapted for running. However, the fact that the holotype skull has a wide forehead and a narrow snout, characteristic of a* T. rex, *and that the skull has some juvenile features leaves some paleontologists doubtful.*

If Nanotyrannus *is its own species, it paints a different picture of the world of* T. rex *and Late Cretaceous. And it also changes the world of Alpha and her pack. Studying Bloody Mary with a* Triceratops *skeleton has caused some paleontologists to look back at other* Triceratops *finds. Some have had scattered teeth around them from unknown predators, perhaps* Nanotyrannus. *By considering the amount of teeth found, it is estimated to have come from ten to fifteen individuals, suggesting that* Nanotryannus *might have been a pack hunter[2].*

Alpha and Beta not only have tyrannosaurs to fear, but packs of Nanotyrannus *as well.*

---

2   *Dino Death Match.*

CHAPTER FOUR

BETA'S CHALLENGER

———

A few months after the run-in with the tyrannosaur, mating season arrives for the raptors. Alpha rests in the shade of a tree. The sun is approaching its highest point in the sky and the raptors are seeking to avoid the hottest part of the day. Her curiosity is peaked. A couple hours ago, an unfamiliar raptor smell found its way to her nostrils. She could tell it was a male, just from the scent.

So could Beta. He is restless and on edge. If the rogue male approaches the pack, he will attempt to win over Alpha and improve his social position. Beta must defend his right as Alpha's mate and his place in the pack.

Alpha is nothing but curious. Love and commitment are not concepts dinosaurs understand. She wants to see the rogue male and also observe his courtship display. More importantly, she wants to see what Beta has to offer to defend his place.

Beta glares down at the bottom of the gully and Alpha watches his arms spread and his feathers stand on end. The smell of the rogue grows stronger. He is here. She stands and walks over to peer down at him.

Life is tough for a lone raptor. They are some of the smallest dinosaurs in their ecosystem and vulnerable to predators when they're not with a pack. In addition, lone raptors are forced to prey on smaller animals like lizards and mammals, as they could never hope to take on the huge herbivores they live with.

As the rogue male approaches, he lets his feathers lay flat on his body and dips his head down, trying to demonstrate that he means no harm. One of the other females in the pack races up to him and dips her head as well, clearly interested in the male. After a quick sniff, he turns away. He knows she is not the alpha.

Alpha keeps her head held high. She is the dominant raptor here and she will show no signs of weakness. This rogue will have to truly impress her if he wishes to stay, but he has a bigger problem to deal with: Beta.

Alpha's mate charges down the slope and snaps his jaws at the rogue. He flinches, but does not become aggressive. Unless he hangs around too long, Beta will not risk injury in an all-out fight.

Instead, Beta stands his body up as tall as it will go and spreads his feathers, becoming almost twice as large as his regular body size.

Alpha takes a couple of steps down, curious about the rogue. He has turned his head away from Beta and has all his attention focused on Alpha. He starts to sway his body back and forth, showing off his feathers in a non-threatening way. This sort of courtship dance allows Alpha to see his strength and decide if he is suitable or not.

She stands still, watching the dance, but she is not persuaded. The dance has shown that the rogue's ribs are visible under his feathers and he lacks strong muscles in his legs.

Beta takes another snap at the rogue male and he backs away, now a little frightened by the bigger, stronger male. Alpha no longer has courtship on her brain. The rogue is now more of a threat and she wants him out of her territory. As quickly as she makes the decision, her feathers stand on end like Beta's and she roars loudly to the sky. The rogue male is frightened, and quickly backs away.

As he approaches the edge of the resting area, Omega timidly approaches him. With only a sniff, he dismisses her. He is no winner himself, but he can tell instantly that she is the lowest member of the pecking order and is therefore uninterested.

The rogue breaks into a run to leave the pack's territory. Beta has saved his position this day, but he knows more challengers will come. However, as he and Alpha bump noses to solidify their relationship, he is not concerned.

As the mating season for the raptors draws to a close, Beta emerges as the victor. Another rogue decided to try his luck and the other male in the pack tried to push his limits, but Beta managed to put him in his place and secure his position in the pack.

A few weeks pass, and Alpha lays a couple dozen eggs and is now charged with the task of guarding them. This means that Beta will be leading most of the hunts from now on and she will remain with her nest. Laying this many eggs is a survival strategy. Some will be eaten by predators, others won't hatch, and some chicks will be too weak to survive. Once disease and predators have taken their toll, Alpha will be left with two or three that will grow to adulthood. They might remain with the pack, be driven out if they become rivals, or be forced to the bottom of the social order.

Years ago, when Alpha was an adolescent, she discovered this pack and attempted to join. Omega was the alpha at the time. The older raptor had never liked her presence, but still tolerated her. Seasons later, Alpha grew into a strong adult through many hunts with the pack, and Omega was growing older. Eventually, Alpha challenged Omega and took her spot. Now the older female has little hope of laying another batch of eggs and is growing skinnier as the seasons wear on.

Alpha's eggs are covered with leaves and branches meant to conceal them from any predator that wanders into the raptors' territory. They also help keep the eggs warm, even though the days are already hot enough. Alpha will spend the next few months laying and sleeping next to the nest, only eating when the pack returns with food.

She might give the task to one of the other females in the future so she can hunt to keep her muscles strong, but the pack will likely not be taking on any huge prey items soon. For the most part, they stick to the smaller lizards and mammals and remain opportunistic hunters.

The eggs finally hatch, and Alpha has fifteen chicks in total. Like modern birds and reptiles, the baby raptors have an egg tooth at the tip of their snout to allow them to break through the shell. It falls off minutes after they are free of the egg.

There are two runts, barely strong enough to stand on their own two feet. The other chicks will feed before they do and they will not live long. Alpha and Beta will not waste their resources caring for them.

Delta also has a new batch of chicks, but not as many as Alpha. She left her nest unattended to go down to the river that runs through their territory and get a drink, and returned to find that her nest had been raided by a lizard and most of her eggs had been eaten. (Although, the lizard did make a tasty snack for her.)

Delta is now left with five chicks, and it is possible none of them will survive the first year of their life. But raptors do not look too far into the future. All in all, with a few yearlings from last year's batch and a healthy new batch, the pack is thriving.

MATING DANCE

A raptor's mating dance could be comparable to that of a modern flightless bird. Raptors are believed to be about as intelligent as one, and so it would follow that their courtship dances would be similar. This process of looking at modern animals to learn about the behaviors of extinct animals is a tool often used by paleontologists to get a picture of what exactly dinosaurs and other extinct animals were doing when they were around.

CHAPTER FIVE

UNDER THE SEA

—

BOREALOSUCHUS

Meaning "boreal crocodile"
Family: Crocodylomorph
Length: 10 feet
Time Period: Late Cretaceous-Paleogene
Similar to modern crocodiles

CHAMPSOSAURUS

Meaning "crocodile lizard"
Family: Crocodylomorph
Length: 5-11 feet
Time Period: Late Cretaceous-Eocene
Similar to modern gharials (crocodile)

MOSASAURUS

Meaning "Meuse River lizard"
Family: Mosasaur
Length: 50 feet
Time Period: Late Cretaceous
Like a giant lizard with fins, apex predator of Cretaceous oceans

HESPERORNIS

Meaning "western bird"
Family: Hesperornithidae (Extinct penguin-like birds)
Length: 4-6 feet
Height: 3 feet
Weight: 20 pounds
Time Period: Late Cretaceous
Bird that lived like a penguin and had a toothed beak

XIPHACTINUS

Meaning "sword ray"
Family: Teleost (Bony fish)
Length: 15-20 feet
Time Period: Late Cretaceous
Jaws almost vertical on head that helped with swallowing prey

CIMOLIASAURUS

Meaning "white chalk lizard"
Family: Plesiosaur
Length: 13-25 feet
Time Period: Mid-Late Cretaceous
Long neck for catching prey; like a sauropod dinosaur with
fins and a short tail

ARCHELON

Meaning "ruler of turtles"
Family: Turtle
Length: 9-13 feet
Time Period: Late Cretaceous
Similar to modern sea turtles, only much larger

A couple months after the new chicks hatched, Alpha leads the pack along with the chicks down to the river to get a drink of water and scout out the herds that might be passing through. It has been a long time since the pack last took down a big herbivore, and Alpha knows they could use the meat.

Alpha and Beta cautiously lead their chicks down to the water while the other raptors get a drink themselves or start to search for herbivores to eat. The chicks number eight now, after a bout of sickness, the death of the two runts, and a snake attack. They walk in-between their parents, unaware of the possibility of danger. A couple of them tussle with each other––they don't know it, but they are practicing for the dominancy battles they will participate in if they live long enough.

Once they are near enough to the river, Alpha and Beta let the chicks go forward to get a drink themselves. The two adult raptors are sniffing the air and scanning everywhere for signs of trouble. They sense nothing. There is a pair of *Nanotyrannus* on the other side of the river, but they are far enough away to not be considered a threat.

Alpha and Beta think they have all their bases covered, but they forgot one thing: to look in the water.

All of a sudden, water splashes into the air as a predator launches itself out at the chicks. It is a *Borealosuchus*, a crocodile. Like modern ones, he was laying in ambush, waiting for prey to get too close, just as the chicks did. He catches two of them in his fourteen-inch jaws, crushing them with his teeth. Their brittle bones snap and they are dead instantly.

Alpha and Beta turn as soon as they hear the splash and start hissing at the *Borealosuchus*, trying to keep him away from the other chicks. They are about as long as this crocodile and much taller, and so the reptile slinks back into the water; however, he has achieved his goal and has something to eat.

Alpha and Beta spend no time grieving. With a hiss, Beta directs the chicks further along the river to avoid the crocodile. Alpha screeches a warning call to the pack, telling them to avoid this spot, though the *Borealosuchus* is most likely full now.

He shares this river with other creatures called champsosaurs, which resemble modern gharials with their thin snouts. Champsosaurs are fish-eaters, however, and try to avoid any contact with dinosaurs, instead opting to swim around in the river and catch fish or occasionally venture out to rest and sunbathe.

This river lets out into the Western Interior Seaway, an ocean that cuts North America in two. Millions of years ago, it stretched up into Canada, but now it is up to the Midwest of the United States. The creatures that live in the water are not dinosaurs themselves, but some have indeed evolved from them. Many of them are even larger than the ones that stalk the land.

The water erupts as one such creature comes to the surface to breathe. His lizard-like head is visible from the surface of the water. He takes a few huge breaths and scans the nearby shore. He can see a school of *Hesperornis*, penguin-like birds, waddling on the rocks and a few more diving into the water. These flightless birds have teeth in their jaws and are much faster in water than on land, swimming around and chasing schools of fish.

The lizard-like creature dives down again. He is a *Mosasaurus*, the apex predator of the oceans. He is about fifty-feet long and could grow even larger if he lives long enough. He resembles a giant lizard with fins and a tail made to propel himself forward in the water.

A scent tickles his nose--the smell of blood. A creature has died and he is hungry. His fins allow him to turn quickly and his tail lashes to get him to his target before a larger mosasaur discovers it. Above him, a school of ammonites floats aimlessly near the surface. They can grow as large as car tires and look like squids with a huge coiled shell on their backs.

The mosasaur notices a couple other predators circling the group of ammonites. These other predators are fish called *Xiphactinus*, and some consider them the ugliest creatures to ever exist. Their jaws are almost vertical on their heads instead of horizontal like most animals. This allows them to swallow prey better, but these ones seem to be learning that ammonites are virtually inedible. The mosasaur carries on, as he learned a long time ago that ammonites are not food. The *Xiphactinus* are not a threat to him. They might head closer to shore and feed on the *Hesperornis* swimming around there.

The mosasaur finally comes across his quarry. An injured *Cimoliasaurus* is lagging behind his pod. *Cimoliasaurus* is a plesiosaur, a descendant of the sauropods on land. Their legs became flippers as they took to the ocean a hundred million years ago. This younger one is about thirteen feet long, but the adults in her pod have grown to about twenty-five feet. They are half the size of the mosasaur and scatter as he approaches.

Sharks had been circling the injured *Cimoliasaurus*. They might have been the ones to cause the injury. They immediately turn and swim away as the mosasaur arrives, as they are much smaller than him.

The *Cimoliasaurus* has no time to be afraid. The mosasaur grabs her in his jaws and she is dead almost instantly. The mosasaur shakes his prey to make sure it is dead and then starts to feed. Skimming the surface of the water above him, a giant turtle called *Archelon* moves away from the kill zone as fast as she can. Even though she is longer than a man is tall, she is far from off the menu for the mosasaur. She takes a few breaths, and then dives and moves on.

AMMONITE ANCESTRY

Ammonites are descendants of a long line of cephalopods. Four hundred and twenty million years before the present day, their ancestors were the top predators of the Ordovician oceans. These creatures, called nautiloids or orthocones, could grow to be as long as an eighteen-wheeled truck with their straight shells. Their only rivals were the eurypterids, the sea scorpions. They came into contact on a daily basis where a fight would often erupt over prey items, such as trilobites and some of the first vertebrates, small fish called Astraspis. *These small fish are the ancestors of all vertebrates, including dinosaurs and humans*[3].

A mass extinction at the end of the Ordovician period pushed the orthocones to the brink and in the next period, the Silurian, they had greatly decreased in size, while the smaller relatives, the coiled nautiloids, had fared well and would eventually grow as large as the ammonites in hundreds of millions of years. Sea scorpions became the dominant predators and began to venture out onto land, the first creatures to do so[4].

MEGALODON

Three million years before the present day, a giant shark stalked waters all around the globe. Possibly growing to be up to fifty feet long, Carcharocles megalodon *was the largest carnivorous fish to ever exist. It existed sixty-two million years after the ancestors of* Megalodon *lived in constant fear of mosasaurs.*

---

3   Jason McKinley and David Connelly, *Animal Armageddon*, Documentary (Digital Ranch, 2009).

4   McKinley and Connelly.

CHAPTER SIX

TRICERATOPS BRAWL

TRICERATOPS

Meaning "three horned face"
Family: Ceratopsian
Length: 26-30 feet
Height at hips: 9.5 feet
Weight: 6-8 tons
Time Period: Late Cretaceous
Three horns and a frill on the head

PACHYCEPHALOSAURUS

Meaning "thick-headed lizard"
Family: Pachycephalosaur
Length: 15 feet

Height at hips: 6 feet
Weight: 1 ton
Time Period: Late Cretaceous
Dome made of bone on top of the head

A few days after the incident by the river, Alpha leaves her chicks in her sister's care and leads the pack out again to find food. In the two seasons since the tyrannosaur encounter, they have only brought down one other young hadrosaur, and Alpha can tell that her pack is ready for something more filling than lizards and mammals.

Following their usual game trails, Alpha holds her head high and sniffs the breeze blowing toward her. There is the scent of a herd on the wind. Her ears pick up the sounds of a battle between two herbivores. She growls to her pack to tell them to follow her. When the battle ends, one of the herbivores might be injured and easy prey for them.

The pack ventures into the forest and Alpha follows her nose and the sounds of the fight to find it. She picks up the pace as she smells blood, and soon the raptors are running through the forest at up to forty miles per hour, faster than anything they share their world with. At the back of the group, Omega struggles to keep up. She is hungrier than the rest and is finding it hard to put strength in her limbs. She starts to fall back, but manages to keep the pack in sight.

Alpha halts at the tree line and looks out onto the plain, immediately disappointed at what she sees. The sound was two bull *Triceratops* exchanging blows. They are adults and they are far stronger than any member of her pack. *Triceratops* have never been food.

The *Triceratops* are known by their distinctive three horns and the frill that shields their neck. Their only problem is that they have no armor from the head back. Blood rushes to the frills of the two bulls as they fight and they turn from dull to more fluorescent colors. They are trying to intimidate each other and seem bigger than they actually are. Neither backs down.

One *Triceratops*, the older one, backs away. He is trying to defend his place in the herd against a younger, stronger competitor. If he loses, he may never be able to pass on his genes again. His instincts propel him forward once again to fight a losing battle. With a sharp, high-pitched call, the younger *Triceratops* meets him, and their horns lock. He is a strong male in his prime. His only disadvantage is that the older bull has more experience.

Unless one of the bulls is severely injured, they will never be a good target for the *Acheroraptor* pack. Alpha turns away from the brawl to find another dinosaur species on the plain. These are *Pachycephalosaurus*, the dome-headed dinosaurs. They are more like the size of the raptors. The *Pachycephalosaurus* are easily distinguishable by the thick dome of bone on the tops of their heads. They walk on two legs, foraging for ferns, oblivious to the danger of the raptor pack at the moment.

Alpha flicks her tail and chirps a little to direct her pack to attack the *Pachycephalosaurus*, when something catches her attention. In the commotion of the confrontation between the two bulls, the herd's ears had been dulled to an approaching threat.

A male *Tyrannosaurus* bursts out of the trees with a deafening roar. He is distinctively male because he is smaller than the females of his species. He is old, with battle scars covering his snout and his eyesight declining. However, his jaws have not weakened. As quickly as he arrives he takes two massive steps to try to corner a young *Triceratops* and have an easy meal. Hunting has been difficult for him ever since his mate died and he was left on his own.

The tyrannosaur is stopped by a bellow from a female *Triceratops*. She raises her horns high and approaches the predator head on. She is completely invulnerable in this position with her frill guarding her neck, and the tyrannosaur is forced to back off from the adolescent.

Alpha and the pack watch as the herd of *Triceratops* all assume a defensive position around the young ones. They stand in a circle with their tails together and their horns facing out, with the young ones in the middle. The tyrannosaur starts to circle them, but he has no opening to attack. The adults stand frill to frill, an impenetrable shield, even against the tyrannosaur's bone-crushing teeth.

The two bulls have ended their engagement and now stand together against the threat of the tyrannosaur. They do not have the protection of the herd. If the tyrannosaur can find a way to flank them and attack from the back or side, they will be much easier prey.

The tyrannosaur hears their grunts of fear and turns in their direction with renewed strength. The speed with which the herd was able to form their defensive line had put a halt to his attack and demoralized him, but now he is ready to fight. He gives a mock lunge, meant to force the two bull *Triceratops* back, and they fall for it easily. While the tyrannosaur is only a little more intelligent than a modern crocodile or monitor lizard, this is clever compared to the *Triceratops*.

After another mock lunge, the younger bull rushes forward, powered by instinct and fear. The tyrannosaur sidesteps his attack and then reaches down to close his jaws around the bull's flank. The *Triceratops* howls in agony.

The older bull seizes his opportunity. He charges while the tyrannosaur is distracted and his horns find their mark in the tyrannosaur's stomach. The tyrannosaur lets go of the other bull as he roars with shock and pain. The older *Triceratops* backs away and the tyrannosaur collapses. He is still alive, but he will not be for much longer, as blood continuously spills out of the wound. It is a disgusting smell to the *Triceratops* and the two males back away.

The herd starts to move off into the forest, trampling undergrowth as they go. They will find another place to feed, far away from the carnage. The older bull follows quickly as the younger one starts to limp in their direction. He is not a threat to the old bull's position of power anymore, not with his injury. He will survive it, but the question still remains if he will ever get his own herd and be able to pass along his genes. He was saved by the older bull, but this is not the reason the other *Triceratops* charged. He did it to save his own life when he saw the opportunity, just as instinct told him to.

With the battle over, Alpha turns back to the *Pachycephalosaurus* herd and is disappointed to see the last ones running off into the forest. She does not want to waste her pack's energy in a chase, not when there's easier prey to find.

She settles down, calling softly to her pack to tell them to rest and wait. She keeps her eyes fixed on the dying tyrannosaur.

The raptors will not dare approach him until he is dead. Then, they will have a feast, as long as nothing else shows up to claim the body.

TRICERATOPS *AND* TOROSAURUS

It has been suggested that another species of ceratopsian, Torosaurus, is actually the adult form of Triceratops. If this is true, then Triceratops could grow to be even larger than previously thought, with the combined head and frill being about nine feet long.

THE DOME-HEAD MYSTERY

It has been suggested in the paleontology community by Dr. Jack Horner that the species Stygimoloch and Dracorex actually represent a juvenile Pachycephalosaurus, a larger dome-headed dinosaur. This is due to the fact that it does not seem anyone has found an adult Stygimoloch or Dracorex. The only problem is the remarkable differences in the structure of the horns on the back of their heads. Some paleontologists have accepted that Stygimoloch and Dracorex are junior synonyms of Pachycephalosaurus and that the ornamentation on the head simply changed with age, but the debate is still out, as there is no evidence of this amount of change among any modern animals[5].

---

5   Brian Switek, "Paleontological Profiles: Jack Horner | Science-Blogs," accessed October 9, 2019, https://scienceblogs.com/laelaps/2008/04/11/paleontological-profiles-jack.

The question also remains if these dinosaurs could have charged at each other and butted heads the way they are often depicted in popular culture, like modern bighorn sheep. Some paleontologists say they would have given each other a concussion if they did that, but others point to the reinforced neck vertebra as evidence that they did. If they did not engage in this behavior, then it is likely the domed head was for mating displays.

At the 2018 meeting of the Society of Vertebrate Paleontology, a new specimen of Pachycephalosaurus *was presented to the paleontologists gathered there, this one identified as a juvenile, and it resembled the skulls of* Dracorex. *What shocked paleontologists were the teeth at the front of its mouth, which had never been found before. They were incisors, resembling those of a carnivore. It is unclear if these teeth were the mark of a juvenile and that the young ones might have been omnivorous and then became fully herbivores by the time they were fully grown, or if* Pachycephalosaurus *was an omnivore even as an adult. Either answer radically changes the picture of Late Cretaceous North America[6].*

---

6   "Vegetarian Dinosaur May Have Actually Eaten Meat, Skull Suggests," Science, October 24, 2018, https://www.nationalgeographic.com/science/2018/10/news-vegetarian-dinosaur-ate-meat-pachycephalosaurus-paleontology/.

CHAPTER SEVEN

SCAVENGER SKIRMISH

———

The sun is starting to sink low in the sky when the tyranno-saur finally takes his last breath. Alpha sees his side go still and her ears no longer hear the sound of his heavy breathing. She opens her jaws to give a call to her pack and tell them to form their ranks. It is time to go in.

Alpha steps out into the clearing with Beta at her shoulder. She sniffs the air, searching for any signs of danger. She and her pack are among the smallest animals in this area and there are many bigger things to fear. She smells something unfamiliar on the wind: another predator.

On the other side of the clearing, a pack of *Nanotyrannus* emerge from the brush. There are four in total, each ten times heavier than an *Acheroraptor* and almost twice as long. They stand up as straight as they can, pulling their necks back and opening their long jaws to roar a challenge at the pack, advancing steadily towards them.

A couple of raptors shift nervously as they await Alpha's orders. She is still, stuck between two decisions. She can run––and the pack can go hungry––or they can fight. Alpha chooses to fight.

Her orange feathers stand up along her spine as she spreads her arms and picks up her small frame to seem larger than she actually is. The pack begins to imitate her as Beta starts to make mock lunges at the *Nanotyrannus* in an attempt to scare them away.

The *Nanotyrannus* are not intimidated––only a little surprised that these little raptors have decided to stand up to them. One of them does not heed the leader's orders. He charges straight at the raptors, hoping to catch a couple of them and crush their brittle bones in his jaws that can clamp down with half a ton of pressure. Alpha and Beta sidestep and execute an attack they and all other raptors have been using for generations. The prey charges in for an attack, they sidestep, and then leap onto either side to confuse and disorient their target.

As the *Nanotyrannus* feels their claws dig into his sides, he backs away, confused that he has missed. He has never encountered raptors before and even his more experienced leader has never fought against them. Alpha extends the claws on her toes and her huge killing claw digs into the side of the *Nanotyrannus*. He roars in pain and starts to shake his body around, hoping to throw the raptors off him. Instead, another follows Alpha and Beta's lead and joins them on the side of the larger predator.

The *Nanotyrannus*'s brain switches from the fight instinct to flight. He turns and runs back to his own pack, causing the raptors to leap off him. They do not want to end up in the middle of the *Nanotyrannus* pack. The smell of blood forces the bigger predators back. They stand their ground against the raptors, but now there is fear creeping into them. The wounded *Nanotyrannus* waits in the back of the pack, wanting the others to protect him. He is now far from able to fight.

Alpha and Beta continue their mock lunges, forcing the *Nanotyrannus* further and further back. Soon, they are pushed beyond the body of the tyrannosaur. The leader of the *Nanotyrannus* pack stands his ground. The fear from the initial attack is gone. With a sharp bellow, he calls one of the others to his side, and then he decides to go for a full frontal assault. They do not waste time with mock lunges.

With their jaws snapping, the raptor pack disperses. None of them get caught in the jaws of the other predators, but Alpha knows they are in a bad spot now. Beta stays by her side, but a couple of raptors are on their own now. The third *Nanotyrannus* races forward and catches one of the raptors in his jaws. The raptor is dead as soon as those jaws close, but Alpha is not ready to give up yet.

She leaps onto the side of the *Nanotyrannus* closest to her, and Beta follows her lead. Following her high pitched screeches, the other raptors mimic her behavior. The *Nanotyrannus* are vulnerable beyond their jaws and at the mercy of the raptors as they dig their killing claws in.

The lead *Nanotyrannus* continues to shift his weight, trying to force Alpha and Beta off him. Alpha loses her grip, falling hard to the ground. She hears the distinct sound of bones snapping as she lands. Her hand is broken and she screams in agony.

Sensing a small weight lifted off him, the *Nanotyrannus* pivots and turns his jaws to Alpha. He doesn't waste a second lunging for the fallen raptor. But Alpha is saved as another raptor, Delta, lands on the neck of the *Nanotyrannus*. Alpha realizes that the other *Nanotyrannus* are in full retreat and the raptor pack is converging on the one remaining predator. Their greater numbers allowed them to overwhelm the larger carnivores.

The *Nanotyrannus* shakes off Delta and then realizes the danger he is in. He charges away as Beta leaps off his side. He and the rest of his pack will be wounded and hungry tonight.

Alpha stands and puts up a show for the pack, especially for the other females. She holds her broken hand close to her body, but shows no sign of weakness. She gives a roar of victory and then turns to claim their prize: the body of the tyrannosaur. At the moment, no raptor will question her authority and she will feast on the most nutritious parts of the tyrannosaur, but with her broken hand, her position as alpha might be in question soon enough.

The raptor pack is not without losses. One raptor was killed by a *Nanotyrannus*, and Alpha's broken hand will weaken the pack if a fight breaks out for her position because of it.

The raptors will not let the body of the fallen member of the pack go to waste. Any sort of attachment they had to this raptor is gone. Now, the body is just part of their dinner.

CHAPTER EIGHT

ANKYLOSAUR INVASION

ANKYLOSAURUS

Meaning "fused lizard"
Family: Ankylosaurs (armored dinosaurs)
Length: 20-26 feet
Height at hips: 5.6 feet
Weight: 5-7 tons
Time Period: Late Cretaceous
Thick armor on back, club on the end of the tail

A couple of nights after the tyrannosaur feast, Alpha wakes from a bad dream. She lets out a small screech as she shakes herself awake. Realizing it was just a dream, she relaxes. She is then annoyed by something that has been disturbing patterns around the world for weeks. She growls at the sky.

A bright light accompanies the moon, making the night even brighter.

IMMINENT IMPACT

What Alpha doesn't know is that the bright light she sees is a six-mile wide asteroid hurtling towards Earth at 20,000 miles per hour. Two giant asteroids collided in deep space during the Jurassic period. This asteroid, a fragment from that impact, has been travelling for almost 100 million years. It has always been fated to strike Earth[7].

The trouble starts when Alpha smells something on the wind. She knows this scent, but she has only seen the dinosaur that carries it once before. She is instantly on edge. She roars to wake up the other raptors and get them ready. The dinosaur approaching is not a predator, but it is something to be feared. It is a dinosaur even a *T. rex* would think twice before attacking.

Lumbering through the gully on short but strong legs is a six ton *Ankylosaurus*. This armored dinosaur is five and half feet tall and completely unafraid of the raptors due to the thick bony armor on its back. Even this dinosaur's eyelids are armored. While the armor is certainly annoying to predators,

---

7   McKinley and Connelly, *Animal Armageddon*.

the thing that truly deters attackers is the club on the end of its tail. Muscles at the base of the ankylosaur's tail allow it to swing with enough force to break bones. While it would break the leg of a *T. rex* and possibly kill it because it couldn't hunt, it would break all the bones in a raptor's body with just a careless swing.

The ankylosaur is in no hurry as he moves through the nesting area of the raptors. His brain is one of the simplest of all dinosaurs and he does not fear predators. In addition, his eyesight is not very good, mainly because he doesn't need it as much. He sniffs the air and smells raptors, but is not afraid of them. He continues onward.

Holding her broken hand close to her body, Alpha stands up and lets out a warning chirp to the other members of the pack as they start to awaken. She does not like this intruder's presence.

The other members of the pack stand at attention, waiting for Alpha's command. She watches as the ankylosaur continues on his way. He raises his head and then turns to make his way up one of the slopes of the gully, which would take him deeper into the raptors' territory. Alpha decides that she cannot allow this. She charges down the slope and gets right in the ankylosaur's face, roaring as loud as she can. The ankylosaur stumbles back, confused at the sudden appearance of the raptor. He has not seen them before. His tail begins to swing back and forth on instinct, where it might catch a predator trying to sneak up behind him.

Most of these raptors have never seen an ankylosaur before, but their instincts tell them to stay away from the tail. Beta, who is standing on the opposite slope from Alpha, growls to tell the raptors with him to stay back. He will not risk one of them being caught by the tail.

Another raptor joins Alpha in her attempt to scare the anky-losaur away. It's working. The bigger dinosaur stumbles back a little ways, disoriented by the mock lunge. He turns away from his assailants and the club on his tail turns as well. Alpha ducks just in time and the club passes right over her head, narrowly missing the other raptor.

The ankylosaur lets out a grunt as he trudges back down the gully and continues on his way. Alpha watches him go until he is out of sight, and then makes her way back over to her chicks. They are a little older and a little bigger now, but still far from adults and need to be protected. Alpha's actions were those of a protective mother and she now settles down next to her chicks.

Beta leads another raptor to follow the ankylosaur and make sure he stays far away from the nesting site.

THE ORIGIN OF ANKYLOSAURS

Ankylosaurs evolved in the early Cretaceous, as new species of dinosaur began to fill the niches left behind as Jurassic period dinosaurs went extinct. One of the earliest was Gastonia, *a much smaller ankylosaurian that lacked the club at the end of its tail.* Gastonia *instead had bony plates that extended off the sides of the tail. They were sharp and could cause devastating damage as the tail was swung from side to side.* Gastonia *was discovered near the largest raptor ever found, named* Utahraptor. *These two creatures lived in the same era and it is theorized that* Gastonia *could have been a potential prey item to* Utahraptor, *leading to confrontations between the two. Both these species were named and described by paleontologist Jim Kirkland.*

CHAPTER NINE

IMPACT

QUETZALCOATLUS

Named after the Aztec god Quetzalcoatl

Family: Azhdarchid (Pterosaur)

Wingspan: 40 feet

Length: 33-36 feet

Weight: 440-550 pounds

Time Peri*od: Late Cretaceous*

One of the largest pterosaurs

The next morning, Alpha is sitting contentedly next to Beta as their chicks scuffle with each other playfully. The *Acheroraptor* pack spends most their day sleeping, like a pride of modern lions. The tyrannosaur provided a good meal for many of them and only now is Alpha starting to feel the pangs of hunger. She might need to lead the pack on another hunt soon.

Her broken hand is not healing and the other females have started to notice. Even Omega is interested in Alpha's weakness. It is not revenge because Alpha stole her position, but just instinct to climb the social ladder. If Alpha needs to lead a hunt, she will also need to lead the first strike, and it may be difficult with her injury. She will need to defend her title soon. If Alpha loses her position, she will also lose Beta, as he would become mates with the new alpha.

For now, Alpha is not worried. Her brain, though intelligent for a dinosaur, is not capable of worrying about future events. She bumps snouts with Beta and then settles her head down to go to sleep.

The light is blinding. It comes as suddenly as lightning during a thunderstorm. Followed soon after is another, even more blinding light to the south. The dinosaurs do not see the asteroid streak across the sky like all our disaster movies imply. One moment everything is fine, and then the next, everything is on fire.

Every dinosaur in North and South America turns their head in the direction of the light. Carnivores stop hunting and herbivores look up from their meals. Everything falls silent as primal birds stop chirping and mammals and insects stop moving to brace for what's coming. The world is about to end.

IMPACT

The first light the dinosaurs saw was the asteroid entering the atmosphere of the Earth and the second is the impact itself. The blast would come later, as sound travels at roughly 767 miles per hour and anything in the immediate vicinity that could hear the impact was dead instantly.

The asteroid struck the Yucatan Peninsula in the Gulf of Mexico, where it gouged a hole 30,000 feet deep and caused the rock of the Earth's crust to behave like a liquid for a split second. The power was equivalent to that of 100 million hydrogen bombs and it was even visible from the moon. The asteroid was vaporized instantly, but the sound it made was deafening when it reached the ears of the dinosaurs

All the water within a 100-mile radius of the impact turned to steam and anything within a 250-mile radius was killed instantly. They could be considered the lucky ones[8].

---

8   Peter Brannen, *The Ends of the World: Volcanic Apocalypses, Lethal Oceans, and Our Quest to Understand Earth's Past Mass Extinctions* (HarperCollins, 2018).

As near as Alpha can tell, there is fire in the sky. Where one second it had been clear, the next there is a trail left behind by the asteroid. She is frozen by fear as other raptors turn to her for direction on how to face this new threat.

There is a monstrous roar not of this world, as super-heated ash and rock race away from the impact zone just three seconds after the impact. Alpha and her pack have only seconds to act.

Millions of years of predatory instinct engraved in her DNA and only one, the most primal, rings true in Alpha's head: *Run.*

Alpha gives no orders and the pack disperses. Some raptors confusedly run in the wrong direction, toward the blast or not directly away from it. Alpha chooses the right way. Instinct tells her to leave her chicks and save herself. She can always lay more eggs.

There is only blinding fear in her brain as she runs as fast her legs can carry her. She has exited the forest that surrounded the nesting site and is now on an open plain. Nothing she or her ancestors have ever faced could have prepared her for this. Anything that was living in the prehistoric Gulf of Mexico or on the surrounding shores had no chance. The dinosaurs farther north, like Alpha, still do.

She ducks into a cave. It has a small entrance, barely big enough for her body to fit through. Instinct tells her that she can only hide from this threat and she has no chance facing it head on.

Something snarls at her from the darkness. Alpha leaps back. She can't go outside, so she decides to face this new theat. She sniffs to figure out what is waiting in the darkness. She realizes it's another *Acheroraptor* and immediately relaxes; she knows this raptor. Omega steps further out into the light and ducks her head.

There's a huge roar from outside as the shock wave of heated rock and ash passes by the cave. Alpha and Omega are blown off their feet by the force, but fare much better than those trapped outside. They are killed as soon as the wave hits them.

After another minute, the shock wave dissipates. Alpha barks to Omega to tell her to be ready. Slowly, with her head down and in a defensive position, Alpha cautiously steps outside with Omega right behind her. The ash still hangs in the air, although it is cooler now. The day has become something like dusk. Alpha can see wildfires burning in a forest not too far away and can feel the heat from here. Forests all across the continent are burning.

Alpha screeches loudly, then pauses and listens for any response from members of her pack, but her call is not answered. The silence is eerie as the landscape is almost devoid of life. She can hear her own heart beating.

Who she really wanted to hear from is one of her chicks, from Delta, or from Beta. It's not love that binds them, only instinct, and Beta has been her mate for too long for her to forget him.

Omega chirps a little, waiting for Alpha's orders. If they were humans, there might be a distaste on Alpha's end for having to work with a lower member of the pack, but this is not the case with dinosaurs. Alpha knows they are much better off together.

All of Alpha's survival instincts are telling her to get as far away from the fire in the sky as possible. Fear has dilated her pupils and sent adrenaline pumping through her veins. Right now, she could run as long as she needs to.

She growls to get Omega to follow her, puts the impact zone to her back, and runs north, with Omega on her tail. But they don't make it far.

The blast has knocked over trees everywhere and Alpha finds herself leaping over them to get further away from the fire in the sky. Before she knows what's happening, she is sent sprawling as the ground starts to shake. She has never experienced an earthquake before and she doesn't know what to do when a magnitude 13 shakes the earth. Omega ends up on the ground next to her, screaming loudly into the sky. The raptors cannot comprehend why the ground they thought they could always depend on has suddenly turned on them, rippling like waves under them. They cannot understand why the ash hangs in the air and the day seems to be turning into night or why they can feel the heat of the wildfires in the distance.

Sixty-five million years ago, this was Doomsday, the day of hell.

The earthquake continues for another twenty minutes and Alpha and Omega are forced to lay and wait for it to stop. When it does, Alpha slowly gets to her feet. The fall hurt her broken hand even more, but other than that she only has a couple bruises. Omega is uninjured as well. After a quick sniff to check, Alpha barks and then the two set off north once again.

As the two raptors run, they start to pant as the impact has turned the surface of the Earth into an oven. And then it starts to rain. This is no normal rain, this is a rain of heated ash and glass created by the impact. It torches the feathers of the raptors as it strikes, causing them to howl in pain. All the dinosaurs who survived the shock wave and the earthquake are now desperately seeking shelter from the rain from hell. Alpha and Omega are fortunate once again when they come across an overhanging rock outcrop. Alpha chirps to get Omega's attention and direct her to the outcrop.

As they make a break for it, the sound of the impact finally catches up with them. The raptors scream in pain as the deafening sound ruptures their eardrums. They stumble into shelter, finding themselves deaf to the sounds of the rain outside.

After taking a moment to calm down a little, Alpha brushes Omega with her feathers, telling her to sit since she cannot give a chirp. They must wait here for it to stop raining glass and for the daytime to come.

A few hours pass and the rain from hell subsides. The night starts to arrive and the two raptors are finally starting to relax as their hearing slowly returns.

Alpha hears sounds from the sky and looks up to see two pterosaurs flying over them, away from the impact zone. She does not fear them, as they are mostly fish eaters. In fact, they would be more terrified of a raptor and would not dare land near them.

A layer of ash is setting over the landscape. Wildfires are still burning, more set off by the rain, but they are a long way from the raptors.

Alpha's eyelids are just starting to feel a little heavy when the last horror on this doomsday rears its ugly head. A heated rock falls from the sky and slams into the ground, startling Alpha and waking Omega, who had fallen asleep with her leader keeping watch. This rock was thrown into the atmosphere by the impact, where it was heated as it fell, and now rocks like this of all sizes are raining back down to Earth.

Alpha hears a screech and looks up to see that a rock has struck one of the pterosaurs out of the sky. The other flies on, not looking back, only at what lies ahead.

Underneath the outcrop, the raptors are safe, but they are frightened by the noises the rocks make as they strike the Earth. Alpha lets out a loud, petrified screech. She has no idea why the world seems to have turned against her.

THE TANIS SITE

Unknown to the raptors, the earthquake did more than cause dinosaurs to stumble. In addition to causing entire forests to fall, it is theorized that it might have played a part in setting off volcanoes all around the world, most notably the Deccan Traps in India. These super volcanoes might have been close in power to the Siberian Traps, which could have caused the end-Permian extinction, the greatest mass extinction of all time[9].

The earthquake also caused tsunamis on coastlines all around the world as well as smaller events in lakes called seiches. A tsunami reached up into the present United States from the Gulf of Mexico, at least as far as Texas.

One of the most recent discoveries in paleontology is called the Tanis site. A paper published on April 1, 2019, which is ironic timing indeed, described some of the fossils found there where animals might have died only minutes after the asteroid struck the Earth. Fish fossils were found with glass in their gills that might have been formed from the impact. It is also believed that markings found on the rocks, which are usually connected with tsunamis, were actually caused by a seiche because the site is further inland and would have been 65 million years ago[10].

There have been claims coming out of that site of discoveries such as a Triceratops *fossil with preserved skin impressions, which seems much too good to be true. There are theories that dinosaurs might have been on the decline or even gone extinct*

---

9   Brannen.
10   Robert DePalma et al., "A Seismically Induced Onshore Surge Deposit at the KPg Boundary, North Dakota," *Proceedings of the National Academy of Sciences of the United States of America*, April 1, 2019, https://learn.rochester.edu/bbcswebdav/pid-1817535-dt-content-rid-21771070_1/courses/EES207.2019SPRING.86155/19-04-01%20-%20 DePalma%20et%20al%202019%20PNAS.pdf.

before the asteroid struck, and this is supported by a small gap in the rock record between where dinosaur fossils are found and the K-Pg boundary that marks the end of the Cretaceous period. Very few fossils have come out of this layer. If a dinosaur fossil has been found at the Tanis site, then this is concrete evidence that dinosaurs were around when the asteroid hit. However, the paper published in 2019 makes no mention of any dinosaur fossils, and so the issue is still up for debate[11].

PTEROSAURS

Pterosaurs evolved at around the same time as dinosaurs, but are not dinosaurs themselves, and have ruled the skies ever since. Birds evolved in the early Cretaceous, but they were small and unable to challenge the pterosaurs, the biggest of which was Quetzalcoatlus *with a forty-foot wingspan. Some had ornamental crests on their heads or on their beaks. The earliest ones had teeth but the later ones lost them, and so it is theorized that they were fish eaters. Some might have even had a feather-like coating on their bodies, but their wings were made of a thin layer of skin, stretched over their hands with a long last finger, resembling a bat's wing. Pterosaurs went extinct at the same time as dinosaurs, and many paleontologists are still unsure why.*

---

11   Michael Greshko, "These Fossils May Capture the Day the Dinosaurs Died. Here's What You Should Know.," Science, March 31, 2019, https://www.nationalgeographic.com/science/2019/03/fossils-found-from-day-dinosaurs-died-chicxulub-tanis-cretaceous-extinction/.

CHAPTER TEN

THE MAMMAL COLONY

———

PURGATORIUS

Named after Purgatory Hill in Montana, where it was discovered
Class: Mammal
Length: 6 inches
Weight: 1.3 ounces
Time Period: Late Cretaceous-Paleocene
Possibly earliest known primate

LYSTROSAURUS

Meaning "shovel lizard"
Order: Therapsid (mammal-like reptile)
Length: 3-8 feet, depending on species

Weight: 100-200 pounds
Time Period: Late Permian-Early Triassic
Two tusks and a beak-like mouth

GORGONOPSID

Order: Therapsid (mammal-like reptile)
Length: 10-16 feet
Height: 3-6 feet
Weight: 1,100-1,500 pounds
Time Period: Late Permian
Apex predator, first saber teeth

SCUTOSAURUS

Meaning "shield lizard"
Family: Pareiasaur
Length: 6.5-10 feet
Height: 4-6 feet
Weight: 1 ton
Time Period: Late Permian
Bony plates on back

Alpha and Omega have survived Doomsday, but so did most of the world. The dinosaurs in Asia and Africa have no idea of the hell on Earth that took place in North America. The real extinction is still to come.

Two days after the asteroid struck, Alpha and Omega have stopped heading north as the fire in the sky has died out. They have been struggling to find any other sort of life. Many forests have burned down and many dinosaurs have died. They have found multiple bodies and have full bellies from feeding on them. They've seen a few lone herbivores. It seems the herds have broken up just as Alpha's pack did.

Alpha noticed last night that the light in the sky is gone. It does nothing to reassure her.

It's on this day that Alpha and Omega have unwittingly come across a colony of prehistoric mammals called *Purgatorius*. The extinction seems to be favoring these little mammals. They are burrowers, which helps them to avoid the much larger dinosaurs and to form a community to help with raising the young and with gathering food. This also allowed them to avoid the shock wave and prosper where the dinosaurs are falling.

Purgatorius is a minimalist and an opportunist. They will eat whatever they can find, and it doesn't take much to feed their smaller bodies. Their behavior is almost like a modern shrew. They also have short lifespans, meaning most of them haven't seen raptors before. They are not afraid of most dinosaurs, but raptors are much closer to their size, and they know they might be on the menu.

When Alpha emerges from the shadow of the trees into a clearing and comes face-to-face with the dominant male, they both go rigid, not exactly sure what to do with each other. Alpha has seen mammals, but not this particular species. She is more curious than hungry at this point. She slowly leans forward, sniffing to catch the scent of this unfamiliar creature.

Skittishness has kept mammals alive for millions of years. The dominant male's instincts take over and he darts down into a burrow. Alpha races over to see the hole and the scent of the little mammals fills her nose. She wouldn't mind having a little snack before she and Omega look for a real dinner.

Another *Purgatorius*, a mother, climbs halfway out of a hole to see what all the commotion is about. Alpha hears the scuffling and turns around to see the female. This time, she doesn't wait to lunge. The *Purgatorius* is quicker, and she vanishes into her burrow. She runs over to her young, just born yesterday, and sweeps them next to her belly.

Alpha presses her ear to the ground and can hear the mammals scuffling as they move through the tunnels. She hears a squeak and lunges blindly, but her teeth close on empty air. The mammal escaped again. Soon they begin to coordinate to wear Alpha out as much as they can.

Omega arrives in the clearing a minute later and sees Alpha chasing the little mammals around. A confused growl escapes her. If she had a sense of humor, she would've thought it amusing to see her leader chasing these mammals around who are so obviously playing with her.

Alpha hears her growl and stops. Instinct tells her to leave the mammals alone. She's already wasted too much energy chasing them, more than she would gain by catching and eating one.

Alpha and Omega move on and all the mammals live to fight, or rather confuse, another day.

MAMMALS VERSUS DINOSAURS

Mammals evolved at around the same time as dinosaurs in the mid-Triassic period. Their ancestors were once the dominant life forms on Earth. Creatures called synapsids, or mammal-like reptiles, were the largest things on Earth in the Permian period, before the Triassic. At that time, a smaller subsect of synapsids called therapsids were the most common. Herbivores called Lystrosaurus *lived in herds that could have numbered in the thousands. They were short, stout animals with tusks on either side of their jaws and a beak-like mouth. They were hunted by a predator called* Gorgonopsid, *a mammal-like reptile that had the first saber teeth, two elongated incisors on either side of its jaw. They were not nearly as long as the teeth on the saber-tooth cats that would come millions of years later, but still impressive nonetheless. The ancestors of snakes and lizards, called eosuchians, and anapsids, turtle relatives like* Scutosaurus, *shared their world. The Permian period also gave rise to the archosaurs, the ancient ancestors of dinosaurs*[12].

The end-Permian extinction was the greatest of all mass extinctions, wiping out over ninety percent of species. That extinction seemed to favor the archosaurs, although the mammal-like reptiles managed to survive as well, including Lystrosaurus. *While the end-Permian was the beginning of the end for the dominance of mammal-like reptiles, it was another mass extinction at the end of the Triassic period that allowed dinosaurs to take over. Mammals were pushed to the shadows, never growing larger than an opossum. They survived all throughout the reign of the dinosaurs for 160 million years*[13].

Mammals are defined by their jaw structure, and paleontologists can tell a lot by examining their teeth. Late Cretaceous mammals had very primitive designs for mammal teeth, so much so that they're not quite fully mammal. Some might have been egg-laying, and there is some question as to whether placental and live-birth mammals had evolved yet.

---

12   *Walking with Monsters: Life Before the Dinosaurs*, Documentary (BBC, 2005).

13   McKinley and Connelly, *Animal Armageddon.*

Mammals did have some advantages over the dinosaurs. They had a precise bite and even egg-laying mammals make milk, which meant they took better care of their young. Dinosaurs also became adapted to very specific lifestyles.

Purgatorius *is considered an ancestor of modern primates, including humans. It is still up for argument whether* Purgatorius *represents the earliest primate or if it was actually part of a sister group. Either way, it is still an important animal in discussing the evolution of primates.*

CHAPTER ELEVEN

A CLASH OF TITANS

THESCELOSAURUS

Meaning "wondrous lizard"
Family: Hypsilophodont
Length: 8-15 feet
Weight: 200-600 pounds
Time Period: Late Cretaceous
Primitive ornithopod that traveled in herds

ALAMOSAURUS

Meaning "Ojo Alamo lizard"
Family: Sauropod (long neck)
Length: 98 feet
Time Period: Late Cretaceous
Titanosaur, largest dinosaur known from North America, esti-
mated from juvenile skeletons

BRACHIOSAURUS

Meaning "arm lizard"
Family: Sauropod (long neck)
Length: 70 feet
Height: 30 feet
Weight: 62 tons
Time Period: Late Jurassic
One of the tallest dinosaurs

CERATOSAURUS

Meaning "horn lizard"
Family: Ceratosaur
Length: 20 feet
Height: 10 feet
Weight: 1,100 pounds
Time Period: Late Jurassic
Only known carnivorous dinosaur with a horn on its nose

ALLOSAURUS

Meaning "different lizard"
Family: Allosaur
Length: 30 feet
Height at hips: 12 feet
Weight: 2-4 tons
Time Period: Late Jurassic
Apex predator of the Jurassic

TORVOSAURUS

Meaning "savage lizard"
Family: Megalosaur
Length: 33 feet
Weight: 4-5 tons
Time Period: Late Jurassic
Competed with Allosaurus

ARGENTINOSAURUS

Meaning "Argentine lizard"
Family: Sauropod (long neck)
Length: 72-110 feet
Weight: 60-110 tons
Time Period: Mid Cretaceous
Possibly the largest dinosaur ever discovered

GIGANOTOSAURUS

Meaning "giant southern lizard"
Family: Carcharodontosaur
Length: 40 feet
Weight: 6-9 tons
Time Period: Mid-Cretaceous
Could have fed on Argentinosaurus

A week after the impact of the asteroid, there's a new killer on the horizon for all the dinosaurs around the world. The asteroid threw massive amounts of rock, dust, ash, and soot into the atmosphere. Some of it rained back down to Earth on Doomsday, but many of the particles remained in the atmosphere. They have been joined by ash clouds released by volcanoes around the world that have been set off by the impact. All this has spread out over the world, plunging the dinosaurs into a darkness that will last for months.

Alpha is immediately confused when she awakens and it is still dark outside. She rests her head once again, thinking she must have not slept very much. She tosses and turns as her body tells her to get up and move. Her stomach rumbles, and so she decides to forgo sleep and stands up. Omega is already sitting up and chirps a greeting to Alpha. She, too, is confused by the darkness.

Alpha leads the other raptor in search of food, but they don't find much this time. Most of the bodies from the initial blast are either too rotten to eat or have been devoured by other carnivores. Alpha is warm-blooded and so her metabolism is higher than some of the other larger dinosaurs that might have been mesotherms, a mix between warm and cold blooded.

Their day is not impeded by the darkness because of their night vision and their acute sense of smell. They operate normally for the most part and eventually settle down, giving up on food for the time being. Like a modern pack of lions, the raptors spend most of their day sleeping, and when they are not sleeping, they are looking for food.

When Alpha awakens again, it is still dark outside and she is disoriented. She wonders how the night could possibly be this long. She chirps to Omega again to get her to wake up, and then they go searching for food once more. They must continue and not let the darkness get in their way.

They soon come across a small group of dinosaurs called *Thescelosaurus*. They are smaller, more primitive plant-eaters and perfect for soothing the aching bellies of the raptors. They walk on two legs, making cooing noises at each other to communicate much like hadrosaurs. There's food over here, they say. The young ones are near me, no signs of predators. The last one is not true.

With a silent flick of her tail and shift in her feathers, Alpha directs Omega to lunge at one of the older, weaker dinosaurs. These herbivores do not share the raptors' night vision or acute sense of smell, making them easy targets.

Omega crouches low and puts one foot in front of the other slowly. She gathers her legs underneath her and tenses her muscles. She leaps and, like a silent bird of prey, lands on her target. The old *Thescelosaurus* collapses under Omega's weight and the raptor delivers a killing blow to the back of its neck. The small herd panics and races away in different directions, blindly attempting to escape the predators.

Alpha emerges into the clearing, bumps snouts with Omega, and then turns to their meal. It will keep them fed for the day. In this new world, the prey is now at the mercy of the predators.

In the shadows, a *Purgatorius* quietly waits for her turn to eat. She will wait for the raptors to finish, and then scavenge any scraps they leave behind. Mammals like her are omnivores and also have an acute sense of smell, which will allow her to prevail in the darkness.

A couple days after hunting the *Thescelosaurus*, Alpha and Omega don't know it, but they are about to bear witness to a colossal battle unlike anything they have ever seen before.

It starts when the raptors unwittingly cross paths with a herd of the largest dinosaurs in North America. They are called *Alamosaurus*. These sauropods, or longnecks, are traveling at a steady pace, hundreds of tons of rolling thunder across the plains.

Alpha wants to quickly move away from the sauropods. They can't see, for one, and even if they could, they would not care about stepping on and crushing a tiny raptor. She calls to

Omega to get her attention and then turns away to move on when a roar stops her in her tracks. Her night vision can see the shape of a *T. rex* walking toward them. Alpha cowers and starts to back away. She should have smelled the tyrannosaur, but her senses were too overwhelmed by the sauropods.

But luckily for the raptors, this tyrannosaur is not interested in them. His eyes are fixed on a bigger prize. One of the *Alamosaurus* is lagging behind. He is old and battle-scarred and getting sicker by the minute. He is, however, still absolutely massive.

Other tyrannosaurs have found the herd as well and spotted the sick dinosaur. Alpha watches as the first tyrannosaur turns to face another that has approached. They bow their heads to show no signs of aggression to each other and then make low grunts, again showing that they have no interest in fighting each other. Once they establish that the other isn't a threat, they start to advance on the *Alamosaurus*.

Soon, more tyrannosaurs begin to arrive. They are ganging up for the kill. A couple have stepped in to separate the sick *Alamosaurus* from the rest of the herd. They roar as loud as they can and toss their heads, even though the other dinosaurs can't see them. The sound is deafening as the tyrannosaurs continue to roar, and the *Alamosaurus* let out calls of alarm and start to move away as fast as their powerful legs can carry them. They would not fear a single tyrannosaur, but they can tell that this is a group.

One tyrannosaur leaps in for a bite. Her jaws close on the side of the sick and separated *Alamosaurus*, and then she backs away quickly. On instinct, the *Alamosaurus* begins to swing his strong tail, hoping to catch one of the predators by surprise. They see the tail begin to move and quickly step away from it, directing their attacks to the legs of the huge sauropod. The tyrannosaurs are taking a page from the raptors' book for this hunt. Eventually, with enough wounds, the *Alamosaurus* will collapse from exhaustion and blood loss.

Knowing that they will never get a bite of that kill, Alpha nudges Omega, and then they start to move away from the hunt. They are not in a huge amount of danger, but the sight and sound of all the tyrannosaurs makes Alpha uneasy. They will search for something else to kill.

The poor *Alamosaurus* does not have the night vision the predators share. All he sees is darkness. He feels the pain from all of his injuries and more, as more wounds are inflicted. He is surrounded and terrified by the roars of the tyrannosaurs. He will die blind, hopeless, and petrified.

ALAMOSAURUS *SIZE*

What paleontologists previously thought were adult Alamosaurus *turned out to be juveniles. When estimating how big one of these dinosaurs could grow, it was found that they rivaled the South American giants such as* Argentinosaurus *and* Patagotitan. *They were perhaps the largest animals to ever inhabit North America.*

SAUROPODS AND THEIR PREDATORS

Sauropods saw their glory in the previous Jurassic period that ended about 145 million years before the present day. Then, giants such as Diplodocus, Apatosaurus, Camarasaurus, *and the famous* Brachiosaurus *were much more common. Some of the smaller sauropods were hunted by predators like* Ceratosaurus *and* Allosaurus.

Ceratosaurus *was a more primitive carnivore, with four fingers on each hand and eyes on the side of its head, making it lack depth perception.* Ceratosaurus *is easily identified by the blade-like horn on its snout. It is the only known carnivore to have a horn on its nose. The horn might have been used for mating displays rather than as a weapon. It is thought that* Ceratosaurus *would live in mating pairs and might have perhaps mated for life.*

Allosaurus, *on the other hand, was the apex predator of its time, easily stealing the throne from* Ceratosaurus. *Like* T. rex,

Allosaurus *had eyes facing forward, allowing it keep its opponent in front of it at all times. It was also smarter and could have hunted in large packs to bring down huge sauropods.*

Stegosaurus *was another famous Jurassic dinosaur. Paleontologists are still unsure of the exact function of the plates on its back. They could have been used as a way to regulate body temperature or serve as a defense against predators. Its main defense mechanism were the four long spikes at the end of its tail.*

Allosaurus *bones have been found with puncture wounds from* Stegosaurus *spikes. This is proof that* Allosaurus *hunted* Stegosaurus *and the two came into conflict with each other. Not only that, but some puncture wounds have been partially healed, with bone starting to fill them. This shows that some* Allosaurus *survived the conflicts, even after being wounded.*

Allosaurus *had an interesting relationship with another carnivore called* Torvosaurus. *In North America, the species of* Allosaurus *was bigger and would out compete* Torvosaurus. *In Europe, it was the other way around. The species of* Torvosaurus *was larger and would out compete* Allosaurus[14].

---

14 *Dinosaur Revolution*, Documentary (Discovery Channel, 2011).

GIANTS OF SOUTH AMERICA

In Cretaceous South America, the giant dinosaur Argentinosaurus *lived in the same time and place as a predator that rivals* T. rex *in size:* Giganotosaurus. *It is thought that a large group of* Giganotosaurus *might team up to take on one of the giant sauropods, like a pride of modern lions to attack an elephant. And so,* T. rex *might have done the same against the large herbivore it lived with.*

THE ORIGIN OF T. REX

T. rex *evolved in Asia––China, to be exact. There, it would have had to hunt massive sauropods and bigger duckbills than in North America.* T. rex *crossed the land bridge between the two continents and migrated to North America a few million years before the asteroid struck the Earth. It had no competition in North America and easily rose to the top of the food chain. If the opportunity presented itself, a* T. rex *would not say no to hunting an* Alamosaurus.

CHAPTER TWELVE

OMEGA

ORNITHOMIMUS

Meaning "bird mimic"
Family: Ornithomimid (ostrich dinosaur)
Length: 12 feet
Height: 6 feet
Weight: 400 pounds
Time Period: Mid-Late Cretaceous
Bipedal and could run as fast as raptors; possibly covered in feathers

It is now two weeks since darkness fell across the globe. Alpha and Omega are content with the new situation. In fact, predators all over the world are doing well. Their acute sense of smell allows them to find prey among the dead and dying herbivores who are suffering from starvation. The herbivores cannot smell as well as the predators and are relying on bumping into some food to be able to eat. And there is another problem.

With the layer of ash and dust in the atmosphere blocking the sun, plants are also starting to die. This includes plankton on the surface of the ocean. Many of them have died and it has thrown off the entire food chain of the ocean. The once mighty mosasaurs are now starving.

Back on land, Alpha and Omega are resting comfortably next to a rock that shields them from the wind. Alpha preens her feathers and checks her injured hand. She can tell that it is healing as it does not hurt as much and she has regained some use of her three fingers. She is lucky to have survived this long, and it is only because of Omega.

The older female lies sleeping next to Alpha. She never once questioned the other raptor's authority. Her survival instincts had kicked in and she had known that going after Alpha could spell doom for the both of them if they were both injured over a petty dominance battle. But the loss of the sun has been hard on her, even more so than Alpha. She is adjusting, and mostly thanks to relying on Alpha's authority. They need each other.

Alpha's mind occasionally wanders to the pack she ran away from on Doomsday. Her sister is probably dead. Delta had been trying to take her chicks along and had not abandoned them like Alpha. It meant none of them survived. There's no way Alpha's chicks could have survived, not without another raptor, even if one had found shelter from the blast. Alpha does wonder about Beta, though. He had run away as well and they had gotten separated in their panic.

Could he still be out there somewhere? Alpha cannot waste energy looking for him.

She is snapped back to reality when the sounds of herbivores catch her attention. She hears the low grunts and moos of a *Triceratops* herd. Their stomping is enough to wake Omega from her doze.

Alpha watches them pass by through the forest, completely unaware of the raptors sitting there. Omega starts to stand, but a noise from Alpha stops her. These *Triceratops* pose no threat to them, so there is no reason to move away.

Alpha can see some of them lagging behind, the young and sick. There are few adults left in the small herd, and they are far from healthy in the way their bones are poking out on their sides and their ribs are visible. Some of them have not eaten in a week and it is a wonder they haven't collapsed yet.

If they did, the herd would not slow down.

Alpha is put on high alert when she smells something else on the wind. She hears the thrumming of hundreds of feet on the forest floor. She becomes a little more relaxed when she recognizes the scent. A herd of *Ornithomimus*, ostrich dinosaurs, pass by the *Triceratops* herd, picking up speed as they go. They would be easy targets because they don't have any body armor, but they match the speed of the raptors. Only an ambush attack would allow a predator to catch them.

Alpha can smell something else besides the herbivores. She can hear the grunts and the roars of other predators. A pack of *Nanotyrannus* is approaching fast. They must have been the ones to spook the *Ornithomimus*, and they seem to have already selected their target among the *Triceratops* herd.

Omega has smelled them, too. She stands up quickly. Alpha screeches to her to get her to start moving. They don't want to be caught in the middle of the hunt. Her screech alerts the *Triceratops*, who swing their massive heads away from the fleeing *Ornithomimus*, but they are not afraid of the raptors, simply surprised that they were so close. If anything, Alpha's screech caught their attention long enough to help the *Nanotyrannus* sneak up on their quarry.

With a roar, the pack bursts forward and launches themselves at one of the sick *Triceratops*. She used to be a healthy adult, but now her hunger has left her vulnerable to disease. She is now an easy target, and the predators sense it.

The attack causes the rest of the herd to panic. They use whatever strength they have left to run in every direction in their attempt to evade a predator they cannot see. In their attempt to escape, some end up injuring themselves or each other. One *Triceratops* runs straight into a tree and is dazed. Another trips and lands heavily on the ground. She might not be able to get up again. One runs straight into the side of one of her herd mates. Her horns pierce the other's side, causing blood to gush out of the wounds. The injured *Triceratops* roars in pain. The heavy smell of blood in the air only drives the others to panic more, in addition to the screams from the *Triceratops* being brought down by the *Nanotyrannus* pack.

Alpha and Omega run in the opposite direction, where she thinks none of the *Triceratops* will go.

She is wrong.

One of them comes charging right at them.

Alpha screams a warning to Omega and then veers out of the way of the charging herbivore approaching like a freight train. Omega takes the time to look back and see what Alpha was warning her about. She tries to move away, but it is too late. The *Triceratops* runs her down without even breaking stride.

Alpha can hear the snap of Omega's brittle bones as the *Triceratops* gallops on. Omega didn't even have time to screech.

Alpha returns to where Omega lies. She doesn't have much hope that the other female survived. She sniffs Omega's feathers and finds only the stench of death. Omega died quickly and without pain, only a little fear as she saw the huge herbivore charging.

The *Nanotyrannus* never slow their attack through all the commotion. The *Triceratops* collapses and they move in to feast. Wanting to get away from the bigger predators, Alpha turns away from Omega's body and moves on. She is not sad over Omega's death as she does not have the brain capability to mourn, but she will find she misses the company of another raptor as she is forced to face the extinction alone.

CHAPTER THIRTEEN

EGG THIEF

It is now a full month and a half since the asteroid impact, and Alpha is no longer seeing large herbivores. Starvation has finally taken just about all of them. In fact, all the herbivorous dinosaurs are gone.

Alpha is beginning to starve, only being able to snack on the small creatures she manages to catch.

Life was always tough for a lone raptor, but it is even worse now. Alpha has not seen any of her own kind since Omega died, and so when she catches the scent of other *Acheroraptor* on the wind, she grows a little excited. But she doesn't recognize them as members of her pack, and so she realizes she must approach them cautiously.

The food chain around the world is beginning to collapse on itself. Large predators like the tyrannosaurs will fall first, as they need a massive amount of food to keep going. Smaller raptors still have a few months left, but as the destruction has been worse in North America, Alpha is feeling the pangs of hunger.

In addition to hunger, there is a new obstacle for the carnivores.

The asteroid impact and the volcanoes released a chemical called sulfur dioxide into the atmosphere. There is enough of it now that it begins to block heat from the sun. Global temperatures plunge.

When the first snow fell, Alpha was intrigued, as she had never seen snow before. She ran around and leaped into the air to catch the snowflakes. She was surprised to find it cold on her tongue. But when she woke up the next morning, there were snowdrifts all around her, meaning she had to push through them to move. Her annoyance began to outweigh her curiosity. This is how she has been forced to live for weeks, just another obstacle as she searches for a declining supply of food, and now as she sneaks up on the new raptors. The cold does not bother her as she is insulated thanks to her feathers.

She crouches beside a rock as the other *Acheroraptor* come into view. From their smell, she identifies them as a male and a female. She watches as the male approaches the female sitting on the ground. He drops a small mammal in front of her and backs away, indicating he caught it for her to eat. She begins to rip it apart without hesitation. Alpha begins to get into a non-threatening pose to approach them, but then stops as the female stands and reveals what she has been protecting.

The female was sitting on her brood of eggs. There was a small amount of them, only ten in total, as this was probably all the female's body could handle. Alpha's brain flicks off the switch for socialization and turns on another. Instead of company, she has found nutrition. Eggs are always on the menu for raptors, but usually not those of her own species. Now, Alpha needs the calories.

She shifts her position to stay downwind of the raptor pair, not wanting to get caught. The female picks up the small mammal body and moves a small distance away to avoid stepping on the eggs. The male ducks in to grab a couple pieces for himself.

With the other raptors ravenously consuming their small meal, Alpha lunges out of her hiding place. She grabs an egg in her hands and another gently between her jaws. At the sound of her feet in the snow, the female turns around, she and Alpha make eye contact for a single second, and then Alpha turns and runs away. The male screeches in outrage and takes off after Alpha as the female stays behind to guard the remaining eggs, roaring in Alpha's direction.

Alpha finds she is in better health than the male. The other *Acheroraptor* gives up on the chase relatively quickly. He does not want to waste his strength chasing the two eggs when he still has several more to protect and another adult to hunt for.

Alpha continues to run until the other raptors are no longer visible. Then, she sets down the eggs in the snow and digs in. These eggs will keep her going for a few more days.

As more and more carnivores grow hungry, they will resort to cannibalism and egg stealing. Some mothers will even turn on their own eggs.

The problem is that they are accelerating their own extinction by eating the next generation.

Alpha turns to the next egg without hesitation.

CHAPTER FOURTEEN

DAKOTARAPTOR ATTACK

DAKOTARAPTOR

Meaning "thief of Dakota"
Family: Dromaeosaur (Raptors)
Length: 18 feet
Height: 6 feet
Weight: 1,000 pounds
Time Period: Late Cretaceous
One of the largest raptors

Alpha and her pack have always been the hunters. Sure, sometimes they would have to fight a couple *Nanotyrannus* or a *T. rex* might steal their food, but at least they would face the threat together and they usually wouldn't be on the menu themselves.

In this new world, as the darkness that has covered the globe for four months begins to lift, the small carnivores like Alpha can now fall easily into the claws of their bigger adversaries.

Alpha has managed to survive on the odd small meal, like a lizard or a mammal she manages to sneak up on, or stealing eggs from other dinosaurs. Her strength is not what it used to be, but she is still alive. Her broken hand has healed for the most part, but it is slightly disfigured.

A roar splits the air in two. It is a raptor call, but deeper and louder than that of an *Acheroraptor*. Alpha turns and braces herself for a fight. No way she could outrun the other predators now.

The two creatures that approach her are Alpha's worst nightmare. She would rather a tyrannosaur appear over the horizon, because she could at least outrun that predator. Instead, she is faced with a pair of *Dakotaraptor*. These creatures are twice her size and her strength. They don't travel in a pack, even before the extinction, only in pairs or threes. They would have no trouble bringing down a full grown *Edmontosaurus* with their size.

The *Dakotaraptor* have every advantage over Alpha. They have bigger claws and more strength in their arms and legs, as well as a more powerful bite. There's two of them and they encircle Alpha in seconds, cutting off every escape route. Alpha has never felt like prey before, but now she understands how a cornered duckbill feels surrounded by a pack of raptors.

She does have a couple of things on her side. For one, her size makes her more nimble than the *Dakotaraptor*, which might allow her to confuse and disorient them enough to escape. She doesn't need to kill them to win, just escape.

This will be the toughest fight of Alpha's life.

Alpha turns her head to the sky and lets out a desperate screech, hoping there might be any *Acheroraptor* in the area that will answer her call.

There is no answer.

One of the *Dakotaraptor* lunges at her and she dodges out of the way. She leaps onto the side of the bigger raptor and digs her killing claw in. The *Dakotaraptor* howls in pain while the other closes its jaws on Alpha's tail and pulls her off and to the ground.

Alpha tries to recover quickly, but is stopped when one of the other raptors plants a foot on her side and flicks its huge claw into her. Alpha roars again, in pain and as a desperate cry for help. There are no sounds other than the *Dakotaraptor*.

They begin to snap at each other, fighting for who gets the first bite. They know that Alpha can't get away, and so in a sense, they are playing with their food.

Alpha lays down her head, about ready to give up. She is exhausted and starving and her strength is fading. She tries to stand up one last time but is thrust to the ground again, and one of the *Dakotaraptor* closes its jaws around her. Alpha lets out another shriek that ends in one last cry for help.

This time, another *Acheroraptor* voice answers.

Something crashes into the side of the *Dakotaraptor* holding Alpha down and Alpha is freed from its jaws. The other *Dakotaraptor* lunges for her, but Alpha's savior lands on this one's head, clawing and biting. Alpha stands, in shock that she seems to have cheated death for the time being.

The other *Acheroraptor* lands and Alpha finds she recognizes this raptor's scent. It is distinctly male. The other raptor spares her a glance and Alpha does recognize him. It's Beta. He, too, has survived everything the extinction could throw at him, and now he and Alpha have been reunited. They bump snouts, happy to see each other.

The *Dakotaraptor* cut their celebration short. Now with another *Acheroraptor*, Alpha can stand up to them. She roars a challenge, injured as she is. One of *Dakotaraptor* takes the bait and goes on the offensive.

It charges in.

Alpha and Beta separate quickly and then time their leaps so they land on either side of the *Dakotaraptor*. They begin to bite and claw with every bit of strength they have. The larger raptor howls in pain, and then its legs start to buckle under the weight of Alpha and Beta. The other *Dakotaraptor* stands shocked at the offensive of the smaller raptors.

Finally, Alpha and Beta's target falls, wounded and dying from blood loss. The other *Dakotaraptor* turns and runs away, unwilling to lose anything else at the claws of the *Acheroraptor.*

Beta steps back. It is still the alpha's duty to deliver the final blow. Alpha grips the *Dakotaraptor*'s neck in her powerful jaws and crunches down, killing it. She lets out a roar to the sky and Beta joins in after a moment. They have survived Doomsday and the darkness and have dinner for the night.

They will spend the rest of their days together, searching for food until there is not enough for them to keep going. They will push on for as long as they can, but their fate will inevitably be the same as all the dinosaurs.

CHAPTER FIFTEEN

THE SURVIVING MAMMALS

———

It is now a full eight months since the impact of the asteroid. The landscape of North America is unrecognizable. There is almost no vegetation and no living thing in sight.

It will take millions of years for the world to recover. There is life, however, under the ground.

The soil and layer of ash shift. A nose pokes through. The full body of a small *Purgatorius* emerges from her burrow. She pricks her ears. Though none remain, she is searching for the familiar stomps of dinosaurs. She is one of the lucky ones. She was born a year before the impact and stayed in her burrow through all the horrors that followed. It does mean that she will spend the rest of her life checking for dinosaurs and hiding at the smallest of sounds. She will never fully comprehend what has happened.

She darts out and over to where her ears have picked up the sounds of insects scurrying in the soil. She digs with her small front feet and her jaws lunge to catch a small insect in her jaws. She needs to keep up her strength to feed her young waiting for her milk in the nest.

As she runs back over to her burrow, she hears a small chirp from another of her species. She looks up. Three more *Purgatorius* have emerged into the open. From their scents, she can tell they are a mother and her two offspring who are a few months old.

The wind picks up. It is strong enough to move a fallen tree branch slightly from where it rests a small distance away. The two older mammals duck quickly into the burrows. The two younger ones start to follow, but stop suddenly. They are too young to remember the dinosaurs and have been taught by their parents to hide at the first sign of danger. But now their curiosity stays their feet. What have their parents been running from? They sniff the air. There is only the smell of their own species.

Their parents will continue to act like this for the rest of their lives, but the new generation will start to act differently. For now, they have almost nothing to fear.

The younger mammals do start a little when a bird lands a small distance away. The few bird species that survived are the only remaining dinosaurs. This small one starts to peck at the soil where the first *Purgatorius* found the insect. The mammals know they have nothing to fear from this bird.

BIRDS SHALL INHERIT THE EARTH?

About forty-five million years before modern times, twenty million years after Doomsday, relatives of Purgatorius *were still small and scurrying around the forest floor of a now recovered Earth. The biggest mammals at that time were sheep-sized. Relatives of horses feasted on the plants growing low to the ground and the earliest whale ancestor swam in the lakes nearby. But the true horror was the thing that stood nine feet tall and ran faster than anything else at the time. This was* Gastornis, *the first "terror bird."*

It is thought that Gastornis *was the top predator of the Eocene, the epoch of the Cenozoic era the world will be in twenty million years after the dinosaurs. It fed on the small horse relatives and scared away any smaller mammals. It was the one and only time that birds ruled the planet as apex predators. However, recent studies have challenged this claim.* Gastornis *and all the other early terror birds might have in fact been herbivores. This is due to the shape of their reconstructed beaks being similar to that of modern herbivorous birds*

For now, the mammals and the bird have no quarrel with each other. A chirp from their mother calls the young into the burrow. The first female is now curled with her young, letting them suckle at her belly.

The number of lives lost in the extinction is incomprehensible. The oceans are empty save for the occasional small school of fish and a shark here and there. The giant mosasaurs, the ammonites, and all the other marine reptiles are gone. Birds now rule the skies, for the huge pterosaurs have vanished as well. On land, crocodiles, lizards, turtles, and frogs have survived the extinction and will live on to the present day.

But *Purgatorius* is the animal that will pave the way for a new era in sixty-five million years. Only one in eleven mammal species survived, but *Purgatorius* is one of the ones that did, the earliest relative of primates. This female's colony will prosper. She will mother many more generations before the end of her life. One hundred years from now, mammal populations will boom.

In millions of years, they will grow to fill every niche the dinosaurs once occupied. The phrase "'the meek will inherit the Earth'" will hold true. The crater that marks the end of the Mesozoic will be underwater.

EPILOGUE

———

If not for the impact of the asteroid, it is possible that dinosaurs would still exist on Earth. They dominated for more than a hundred million years and there is little evidence that they wouldn't have continued their reign. There is some suggestion that dinosaurs were starting to decline even before the asteroid hit, but there had been a slump like this before in-between the Jurassic and Cretaceous periods and dinosaurs had recovered then.

Some paleontologists are still unsure what drove all the non-avian dinosaurs, pterosaurs, and marine reptiles to extinction. With the herbivores and large carnivores, it makes sense. But smaller carnivores, like the raptors, should have been able to get by, as well as smaller species of pterosaurs.

Why they went extinct and birds survived is still a mystery.

In the oceans following the impact, the mighty mosasaurs, the giant turtles, ammonites, and all marine reptiles like *Cimoliasaurus* were gone. Only sharks and schools of small fish remained. The impact wiped out over 98 percent of living plankton, leaving a relatively small amount of individuals to repopulate. In the following years, mammals would take to the water to become whales.

All in all, the extinction claimed 80 percent of living species, leaving only fossils that would later be dug up and placed in museums. Part of the wonder of them that captures paleontologists is that no human has ever and probably will never see one alive. There is much to be learned from these creatures and the factors that drove them to extinction.

It should also be noted that the events described in this story not only describe the past, but could represent the future. The asteroid threw ecosystems into disarray not from the impact, but by setting off volcanoes around the world and causing a large amount of greenhouse gases to enter the atmosphere. This is the same thing humans are doing by burning fossil fuels and if nothing is done about this soon, the Earth could face a sixth mass extinction greater than any before.

Next time you find yourself near a natural history museum, go in. Seek out the exhibits that display extinct animals. Look at the skeletons and imagine them alive. Think of the noises they might have made, what color they could have been, and how they would have lived. This is what paleontologists strive to learn.

In the Smithsonian Museum of Natural History, there lies two fossils in a glass case with the name *Acheroraptor* next to them. If you ever have the chance, go see them. You will find the ends of the upper and lower jaws along with a few teeth. Imagine that these fossils belonged to Alpha and remember her journey and the story of the end of the dinosaurs.

ACKNOWLEDGEMENTS

———

I have wanted to publish a book for as long as I can remember. I filled up notebook after notebook with stories as a kid and I have too many documents saved on my computer of stories waiting to be finished. *Alpha* was one of them, and thanks to these incredible people, my dream has come true.

First and foremost I want to thank my parents, my grandparents, and my Aunt Sarah for supporting me every step of the way. I love you guys and this never would have been possible without you.

Thank you to my U of R friends; Zach, Jake, Adam, Jenna, and Anna, for pushing me when it felt impossible to get everything done and for making my college experience awesome. Wouldn't be here without you guys.

Thank you to my high school friends, especially Michael, Nathan, Erik, Jared, and Dante, for making it through Red Jacket with me and helping me get to where I am today.

A special thanks to my editors; Cynthia Maloy, Heather Gomez, and Kayla LeFevre. Thank you guys for reading all 20,000+ words multiple times and I hope you all feel as attached to this story as I do.

Thank you Brian Bies and Eric Koester for this amazing program and giving me the opportunity to participate in it.

An amazing thank you to the people I interviewed, who set aside time in their busy schedules to speak to me in person, over the phone, or send an email response to my questions.

Thank you to my high school teachers Mrs. Liberati and Mr. Ott. Thank you Mrs. Liberati for giving me the opportunity to create this story and reading not one but two drafts, and Mr. Ott for taking the time to have an interview with me and for buying a book.

And thank you to everyone who pre-ordered the eBook, paperback, and multiple copies to make publishing possible, helped spread the word about *Alpha* to gather amazing momentum, and helped me publish a book I am proud of. I am sincerely grateful for all of your help.

Lana Schultz

Heather Baxter

Marcy Daniels

Nathan Ester

Stacy Liberati

Mr. & Mrs. Raulli

Erica Raulli Giardino

Chyanne Harrison

Cindy Handley*

Lisa Lombardi

Roxie O'Brien

Jim Schneider

Leasa Vacarella

Lori Ryan

Jerry McGee

Joanne Lewandowski

Katie Fish

Tina Altieri

Joanne Miller

Kathy and Dale Fish

Brad Malone

Mark and
Shannon Colangelo*

Charlene Dehn

Peter Bachison**

Eric Cottrell

Vector Zhang*

Joe Marciante

Michael Samodurov

Marisa and JJ*

Alyssa Garner

Abbie Van Wely

Harold Clark

~Randall Ott*

Dawn Mahan

Charmaine Heffner

Laura Frey*

Heather Bachman

Anna Mercer

Sarah Mitchell

Ron and Lisa Baley

Christine and Todd Hardy

Doug and Erin Schneider

Andrew and Lori Warner*

Dolores Colangelo

Isabelle Kearney

My parents (Mike and Rebecca Schneider)***

My grandparents (Ron and Mickie Mitchell)****

My grandparents (Steve and Barbara Schneider)

Key: *two copies purchased, **five copies purchased, ***ten copies purchased, ****twenty-five copies purchased, ~featured interviewee

APPENDIX

Brannen, Peter. The Ends of the World: Volcanic Apocalypses, Lethal Oceans, and Our Quest to Understand
Earth's Past Mass Extinctions. HarperCollins, 2018.

DePalma, Robert, Jan Smit, David Burnham, Klaudia
Kuiper, Philip Manning, Anton Oleinik, Peter Larson,
et al. "A Seismically Induced Onshore Surge Deposit
at the KPg Boundary, North Dakota." Proceedings of
the National Academy of Sciences of the United States
of America, April 1, 2019. https://learn.rochester.edu/
bbcswebdav/pid-1817535-dt-content-rid-21771070_1/courses/
EES207.2019SPRING.86155/19-04-01%20-%20DePalma%20
et%20al%202019%20PNAS.pdf.

Dino Death Match. Documentary. National Geographic, 2011.

Dinosaur Revolution. Documentary. Discovery Channel, 2011.

Greshko, Michael. "These Fossils May Capture the Day the Dinosaurs Died. Here's What You Should Know." Science, March 31, 2019. https://www.nationalgeographic. com/science/2019/03/fossils-found-from-day-dino-saurs-died-chicxulub-tanis-cretaceous-extinction/.

McKinley, Jason, and David Connelly. Animal Armageddon. Documentary. Digital Ranch, 2009.

Switek, Brian. "Paleontological Profiles: Jack Horner | ScienceBlogs." Accessed October 9, 2019. https://scienceblogs. com/laelaps/2008/04/11/paleontological-profiles-jack.

"Vegetarian Dinosaur May Have Actually Eaten Meat, Skull Suggests." Science, October 24, 2018. https://www. nationalgeographic.com/science/2018/10/news-vegetari-an-dinosaur-ate-meat-pachycephalosaurus-paleontology/.

Walking with Monsters: Life Before the Dinosaurs. Documentary. BBC, 2005.